American Christmas Classics

American Christmas Classics

Ronald M. Clancy

EDITED BY WILLIAM E. STUDWELL

CHRISTMAS CLASSICS, LTD.

NORTH CAPE MAY, NJ   2001

Facing page: Bringing Home
the Christmas Tree, *c. 1948*
oil on masonite
Eric Sloane (1910–1985)

For further copyright information, please see page 137

ISBN 0-615-11507-1

Manufactured in Hong Kong

Designed by Adrianne Onderdonk Dudden

To Renate, and so many others who have brought
the light and joy of Christmas into my life.

Part of proceeds from the sale of *American Christmas Classics*
will go to the **National World War II Memorial.**

Contents

Christmas Prayers
1872 oil on panel
Henry Bacon (1835-1912)
Private Collection

December 18 1920   Vol. LXXXV No. 51. Published Weekly at Philadelphia, Pennsylvania. Entered as Second-Class Matter July 7, 1911 at the Post Office at Philadelphia, Pennsylvania, Under the Act of March 3, 1879.   Five Cents the Copy

The COUNTRY GENTLEMAN

The OLDEST AGRICULTURAL JOURNAL in the WORLD

Norman Rockwell

CHRISTMAS

List of Illustrations

Our sincere gratitude is extended to the management and staff of the institutions, museums, private collections, and photo agencies which have made their images available. A thorough, diligent, and good faith effort has been made to identify and then communicate with owners of all images. If errors inadvertently have occurred, corrections will be made in future editions, providing that notification is sent to the publisher.

Facing page:
Christmas
from Country Gentleman,
December 18, 1920
Norman Rockwell (1894-1978)

Norman Rockwell (1894-1978), American, *Freedom from Want*, cover of *The Saturday Evening Post, March 6, 1943*. Printed by permission of the Norman Rockwell Family Trust.   *31*

F. D. Lohman, American, *The Wrong Shall Fail, the Right Prevail*, illustration from "Christmas Carols, selected and arranged by Karl Schulte", © 1942, renewed 1989 Golden Books Publishing Co., Inc., New York. All rights reserved. Reprinted with permission.   *32*

Advertising illustration for Western Electric Company from *LIFE, December 11, 1944*, Courtesy of Lucent Technologies Inc. © 1944. Lucent Technologies Inc. All Rights Reserved. Western Electric is a registered trademark and Bell Telephone Laboratories is a trademark of Lucent Technologies Inc.   *33*

Peter Helck (1893-1988), American, *"Hi ya, soldier!"*, advertising illustration for Pacific Mills, Inc. from *LIFE, December 11, 1944*. Courtesy of Springs Industries, Inc.   *34*

American Christmas card, *Nativity Greetings*, c.1938, Free Library of Philadelphia Print Department.   *35*

John Falter (1910-1982), American, cover of *The Saturday Evening Post, December 3, 1949*, Curtis Publishing Co., Indianapolis.   *36*

William Brantley Van Ingen (1858-1955), American, *The Trombone Choir in the Cupola of the Moravian Church in Bethlehem*, mural from State Capitol of Pennsylvania, Pennsylvania Capitol Preservation Committee, Harrisburg.   *40*

James Bannister (1821-1901), *Martin Luther and His Family at Wittenberg, Christmas Eve, 1536*, engraving after an 1845 painting by Karl A. Schwerdgeburth (1785-1878), German, Evangelical Lutheran Church of America, Chicago.   *42*

Abbott Handerson Thayer (1849-1921), American, *Angel*, 1889, National Museum of American Art, Washington DC/Art Resource, New York.   *43*

American Christmas Card from Louis Prang Co., *Birthday of a King*, 1898, Archives Center, National Museum of American History, Smithsonian Institution, Washington DC.   *44*

Melvin C. Warren (1920-1995), American, *Stranger in Town*. Printed by permission of Mrs. Melvin C. Warren.   *45*

Currier & Ives color lithograph, *Home to Thanksgiving*, 1867, after a painting by George Henry Durrie (1820-1863), American, The Harry T. Peters Collection, 58.300.97, © The Museum of the City of New York.   *47*

Piotr Levchenko (1859-1917), Ukrainian, *Village in Winter*, 1891,Ukrainian National Art Museum, Kiev.   *48*

Print reproduction, *Christmas Chimes*, early 20th century, after a painting by Edwin Blashfield (1848-1936), American, Library of Congress Prints & Photograph Division, Washington DC.   *50*

Illustration from *Ideals Magazine*, December 1953, *Carolers*, © Ideals Publications Incorporated, Nashville, TN. Used with permission.   *52*

Florence Edith Storer (active 1900-1915), American, *Angels Beneath the Tall Tree*, illustration from "Christmas Tales and Christmas Verse", 1912, Annenberg Rare Book & Manuscript Library, University of Pennsylvania.   *54*

Thomas Moran (1837-1926), American, *On Earth Peace Among Men of Good Will*, late 19th

F.D. Lohman, American, *"Peace on the Earth, Good Will to Men"*, illustration from "Christmas Carols, selected and arranged by Karl Schulte", © 1942, renewed 1989 Golden Books Publishing Co., Inc., New York. All rights reserved. Reprinted with permission.   *76*

James Chapin (1887-1975), American, *Ruby Green Singing*, 1928, oil on canvas. Bequest of R.H. Norton, 53.29, Norton Museum of Art, West Palm Beach, FL.   *77*

Mead Schaeffer (1898-1980), American, *Christmas 1943*, cover of *The Saturday Evening Post, December 25, 1943*, Curtis Publishing Co., Indianapolis.   *78*

American Christmas card, *Glad Tidings*, c.1880-1885, Archives Center, National Museum of American History, Smithsonian Institution, Washington DC.   *79*

American antique Christmas card, *Emmanuel*, c.1880-1885, Archives Center, National Museum of American History, Smithsonian Institution, Washington DC.   *80*

John Falter (1910-1982), American, *Falls City, Nebraska*, cover of *The Saturday Evening Post, December 21, 1946*, Curtis Publishing Co., Indianapolis.   *81*

Florence Edith Storer (active 1900-1915), American, *With Babe on Her Knee*, illustration from "Christmas Tales and Christmas Verse", 1912, Annenberg Rare Book & Manuscript Library, University of Pennsylvania.   *83*

Grandma Moses (1860-1961), American, *Joy Ride*, oil on pressed wood, © 1953 (renewed 1981), Grandma Moses Properties Co., New York.   *85*

George Henry Durrie (1820-1863), American, *A Christmas Party*, 1853, The Thomas Gilcrease Institute of American History & Art, Tulsa, OK.   *86*

Advertising illustration for Hamilton Watch Company from *The Saturday Evening Post, December 11, 1943*. Courtesy of the Swatch Group U.S.   *88*

Jon Whitcomb (1906-1988), American, *Back Home for Keeps*, advertising illustration for Oneida Ltd. from *LIFE, October 18, 1943*. © Oneida Ltd. All rights reserved.   *89*

Ezra Jack Keats (1916-1983), American, *The Little Drummer Boy*, 1968, illustration from "The Little Drummer Boy". With permission from the Ezra Jack Keats Foundation.   *90*

Thomas Hart Benton (1889-1975), American, *Sunday Morning*, print. © T.H. Benton and R.P. Benton Testamentary Trusts/VAGA, New York.   *92*

Allan Rohan Crite (b.1916), African-American, *"O' Mary Where Is Your Baby"*, from the series "The Christmas Story", 1942. Museum purchase; prior gifts of Mrs. G. Stewart King, J. Lester Parsons, and Frederick C. Pratt, 1993.30.9, The Montclair Art Museum. © Printed by permission of Jackie Crite, c/o Allan Rohan Crite.   *94*

David Roberts (1796-1864), Scottish, *Church of the Nativity*, 1840, Paisley Museum & Art Gallery, Renfrewshire Council, Paisley, Scotland.   *95*

Norman Rockwell (1894-1978), American, *Little Girl Looking Downstairs at a Christmas Party*, cover of *McCall's, December 1964*. Printed by permission of the Norman Rockwell Family Trust.   *97*

Denver Laredo Gillen (b.1914), American, *Santa Enlisting Rudolph the Red-Nosed Reindeer*, 1939, from "Rudolph the Red-Nosed Reindeer" by Robert L. May. © 1939, 1967 by Robert L. May Company. Used by permission of Modern Curriculum Press, an imprint of Pearson Learning.   *98*

Denver Laredo Gillen (b.1914), American, *Rudolph Joining the Other Reindeer*, 1939, from "Rudolph the Red-Nosed Reindeer" by Robert L. May. © 1939, 1967 by Robert L. May Company. Used by permission of Modern Curriculum Press, an imprint of Pearson Learning.   *99*

Thomas Nast (1840-1902), American, *Caught!*, from *Harper's Weekly, December 24, 1881*, Library of Congress Prints & Photograph Division, Washington, DC.   *100*

Roy Spreter (1899-1967), American, *Children on Christmas Morning with RCA Radio*, RCA-Victor advertisement from *The Saturday Evening Post December 14, 1935*. Photo courtesy of the Archives of the American Illustrator's Gallery, New York City. © 2000, by ASaP of Holderness, NH. Permission courtesy of GE Corp. and Thomson Consumer Electronics, Inc.   *101*

George H. Boughton (1833-1905), American, *Pilgrims Going to Church*, The New York Historical Society.   *102*

Henry Ossawa Tanner (1859-1937), African-American, *Angels Appearing Before the Shepherds*, c.1901, National Museum of American Art, Washington DC/Art Resource, New York.   *105*

Edward Burne-Jones (1833-1898), English, *Annunciation to the Shepherds*, 1864, stained glass panel at The Parish Church of St. Editha's, Amington, Straffordshire (U.K.). Courtesy of Donald G.R. Green.   *106*

John Gannam (1905-1965), American, advertising illustration for Pacific Mills Co. from *LIFE, December 20, 1948*. Courtesy of the Gannam family and Springs Industries, Inc.   *107*

Currier & Ives lithograph after an anonymous American painting, *Early Winter*, 1869, The Harry T. Peters Collection, 58.300.137. © The Museum of the City of New York.   *109*

American Christmas card, *Some Children See Him*, c.1960, Collection of the Free Library of Philadelphia Print Department.   *112*

Lauren Ford (1893-1973), American, *The Nativity Star*, c.1950. Courtesy of Jane Dore Ford Nestler.   *113*

Elihu Vedder (1836-1923), American, *The Star of Bethlehem*, oil on canvas, gift of Mrs. Hattie Bishop Speed, 1938.56, Collection of the Speed Art Museum, Louisville, KY.   *115*

Norman Rockwell (1894-1978), American, *Christmas Homecoming*, cover of *The Saturday Evening Post, December 25, 1948*. Printed by permission of the Norman Rockwell Family Trust.   *116*

Grandma Moses (1860-1961), American, *Christmas at Home*, 1946, oil pressed on wood, © 1955 (renewed 1983), Grandma Moses Properties Co., New York.   *117*

Sheet music cover illustration, *"Babes in Toy Land"*, 1903, Archives Center, DeVincent Collection, National Museum of American History, Smithsonian Institution, Washington DC.   *118*

Sarah Stilwell Weber (1878-1939), American, cover of *The Saturday Evening Post, December 25, 1909*, Curtis Publishing Co., Indianapolis.   *118*

Gentile da Fabriano (c.1370-1427), Italian (Florentine), *St. Nicholas*, 1425, Galleria degli Uffizi/Art Resource-Scala, New York.   *119*

Lorenzo Bicci (1371-1452), Italian (Florentine), *St. Nicholas Resuscitating the Three Youths*, gift of Francis Kleinberger, 1916 (16.121). Photograph © 1993 the Metropolitan Museum of Art, New York.   *120*

Jan Steen (1626-1679), Dutch, *St. Nicholas Gifts*, Rijksmuseum, Amsterdam.   *121*

Theodore C. Boyd (19th century), American, engraving from 1848 publication of "A Visit from St. Nicholas" by Clement Clarke Moore. Courtesy of Mary Pat Myers Photography, Cape May, NJ.   *122*

Thomas Nast (1840-1902), American, *"Merry Old Santa Claus"*, from *Harper's Weekly January 1, 1888*, Library of Congress Prints & Photograph Division, Washington DC.   *123*

Haddon H. Sundblom (1899-1976), American, *Good Boys and Girls*, 1951. This image of Santa Claus is a registered trademark of The Coca-Cola Company.   *124*

John La Farge (1835-1910), American, *The Three Wise Men*, c.1878, gift of Edward W. Hopper, 90.151. Courtesy Museum of Fine Arts, Boston.   *125*

John Falter (1910-1982), American, *New Year's Eve*, cover of *The Saturday Evening Post, January 3, 1948*. Curtis Publishing Co., Indianapolis.   *128*

Grandma Moses (1860-1961), American, *White Christmas*, oil pressed on wood, © 1955 (renewed 1983), Grandma Moses Properties Co., New York.   *129*

Agnes Tait, (1894-1981), American, *Skating in Central Park, 1934*, National Museum of American Art, Smithsonian Institution, Washington DC/Art Resource, New York.   *131*

Thomas Birch (1779-1851), American, c.1840, *A Winter Sleigh Ride*, oil on canvas, gift of Hampton C. Randolph, Sr., Collection of the Brandywine River Museum.   *140*

Acknowledgments

The inspiration for this collection comes from a number of sources, particularly from close friends and family. A great debt of gratitude is owed to the following people and organizations: Charles Sens and other members of the Library of Congress Music Division; current and former members of Free Library of Philadelphia Music Department, especially Linda Wood, Maureen Cattie, Paula Mentusky, Martha Minor, Judy Harvey, and Sidney Grolnic; Marjorie Hassen and her staff of the Music Division of the Van Pelt Library of the University of Pennsylvania; staff members of the Mormon Tabernacle Choir, Salt Lake City; Susan Maurizi of Bethesda, MD, a superb editor who made an immeasurable contribution to this effort; and Prof. William Studwell, a rich resource and well-known authority on Christmas carols.

For helping with the difficult task of assembling the representative images, we are ever in the debt of Adrianne Onderdonk Dudden, a book designer with exquisite taste, and a host of dedicated art librarians, including staff personnel from 1) the Pennsylvania Academy of Fine Arts, Philadelphia, 2) the University of Pennsylvania Fine Arts Library, 3) the Cape May County Library, Cape May Courthouse, NJ, 4) members of the Photographic and Prints Department of the National Museum of American History (Smithsonian Institution), especially Vanessa Broussard-Simmons, Robert Harding, and Dave Burgevin, 5) the Library of Congress Prints & Photos Division, and in particular Sandy Lawson of the Photographic Department, 6) John Pollack of the Annenberg Rare Book Library of the University of Pennsylvania, and 7) the Philadelphia Free Library, including Joe Benford of the Prints Department and Deborah Litwack and her staff of the Art Department.

A professional deserving special mention is John Penn, formerly of SONY Music Special Products, who was ably assisted by his colleagues Dan Rivard, Lucy DeRosa, and Susan Sachs. Years ahead of anyone else from the music industry, John provided continued support for the concept that information, art, and audio music can be effectively fused together as a single package. Also worthy of similar citation is Joel Adams of Devon Consulting of Wayne, PA, whose friendship exceeded all bounds by allowing use of his company's facility and computer equipment, and to his staff members, past and present, including Santi and Ramana Kanumalla, Dennis Pazicni, Sue Bodalski, Russell Calvanese, Marsha Johnson, and Amy Bennett. Jeannie March, Kay Cole, Hank Gehron, Dawne Greth, Jim Sherry, and Joan Berenato also provided immeasurable comfort during the long development stage.

For their faithful and moral support, Mary Ann and Bob Scott of Media, PA, are owed much more than they realize, and the encouragement of Al Kreider, Bill and Bonnie Revaitis, Mike Maurizi, and Terry and Vivan Hogan helped to sustain me over the years. Special contributions were also made by Ms. Elisabeth

"Mausi" Meyers, Anthony Clancy, and the Michael Wozniak family. The greatest debt of gratitude, however, is owed to my wife, Renate, whose love and encouragement provided the needed boost to continue with the project, which, in the estimation of many, seemed to be either an impossible mission or an overly ambitious one.

To varying degrees, these individuals and organizations confirmed the value of team effort, professionalism, and attention to detail. Thus, their efforts have made *American Christmas Classics* a truly collaborative enterprise.

R.M.C.

Preface

With four successful books (*Christmas Carols: A Reference Guide*, Garland, 1985, *The Christmas Carol Reader*, Haworth, 1995, *Glad Tidings: Essays on Christmas Music*, Haworth, 1998, and the text for *The Christmas Card Songbook*, Hal Leonard, 1991), plus over 50 articles and about 200 media appearances on the topic, I have often been described as an expert on Christmas music, and more than occasionally as the leading expert. Yet in spite of all these activities, for which I have received a fair degree of fame and international attention, I have long felt that I had not finished my work on Christmas music. Somewhere in the fuzzy future I had hoped to compile the ultimate annotated collection of Christmas music. I have seen various anthologies of Christmas songs appear from time to time, some of them very good. None of them, however, turned out to be completely satisfying or fulfilling, either musically or psychologically.

While I was still sustaining my vision of the ultimate Christmas collection, I was diverted to other more attainable goals, including annotated anthologies of American state songs, college fight songs, and circus songs. However, when Ronald Clancy recently brought his superlative Christmas project to my attention, I felt a combination of pleasure and relief. The pleasure bordering on ecstasy was caused by his brilliant and even visionary *THE MILLENNIA COLLECTION: Glorious Christmas Music, Songs and Carols* (this volume *American Christmas Classics* is part of that collection), a blend of first-rate and well-written historical information and a broad and very well chosen selection of 170 classical, sacred, and secular Christmas-affiliated compositions. I tried but failed to find any meaningful gaps in the historical coverage and also tried but failed to find any key or important musical piece not in his collection. I also could not find any compositions among the 170 not deserving to be there.

The considerable relief was that I, with more projects than I could possibly achieve in the rest of my life, no longer had the burden of unfulfilled obligations. The project that I might have done sometime was now about to come into full bloom. On top of that, Clancy's exceptional publication is probably better than anything I may have produced. I can take vicarious joy in having even a slight connection with this masterpiece of holiday literature. It is the ultimate Christmas collection, which enhances and complements all my writings and activities on Christmas music and should be a classic for generations!

William E. Studwell, Professor
Northern Illinois University Libraries

Introduction

American Christmas Classics evolved from a planned larger Christmas music product titled *THE MILLENNIA COLLECTION: Glorious Christmas Music, Songs, and Carols*. The latter was born from the simple curiosity of wanting to know more about the origins and development of Christmas music. There were always intriguing questions. When did Christmas music begin? What did it sound like in the early centuries, or in the 13th, or 15th, or 17th centuries? Many books have been published about Christmas music, predominantly carol collections, but there has been no definitive work that traced the evolution of Christmas music from the early years of Christianity to the modern era.

Much ground was covered to answer these questions in *THE MILLENNIA COLLECTION,* and perhaps the reader might want to discover there some of the quite fascinating history of Christmas music. As the collection makes clear, there is considerably more substance to the body of Christmas music than the limited number of traditional religious and secular standards that we are accustomed to hearing repeatedly each holiday season during the course of Christmas shopping, riding in our cars, or just plain relaxing at home. Some of the very best Christmas music actually is performed at various churches or concert halls during Advent, or Christmastide, as part of musical programs staged by professional or amateur groups. These fine works are unfamiliar to many Americans.

When my friends suggested I pursue the idea of writing about the topic of Christmas music, I took their suggestion with a little trepidation, yet in earnest. Ultimately, after years of trial and effort, and despite a slew of rejections from the music and publishing worlds, *THE MILLENNIA COLLECTION: Glorious Christmas Music, Songs, and Carols* had a life of its own, and from it *American Christmas Classics* evolved.

Considering how young the United States is compared with many other countries of the world, particularly those of Europe, American musicians and songwriters have made significant contributions to the Christmas music repertoire and their works energize *American Christmas Classics.* In keeping with their spirit, I tried to keep an eye on the following objectives:

1— to compile a reasonably comprehensive collection of American Christmas songs and carols of both a religious and a secular nature;

2— to include interesting background information, whenever possible, about each of the selections;

3— to provide lyrics for each selection without printing the space-consuming music texts that not all readers can effectively use;

4— to introduce a concise and informative historical perspective about the development of American Christmas music, interwoven with information about

Facing page:
The Nativity, *1912*
oil on canvas
N.C. Wyeth (1882-1945)
Brandywine River Museum

Christmas traditions and customs whenever possible, thus allowing the reader to understand the cultural context of Christmas music and how the compositions might have sounded at given moments in time from the 18th century to the 20th century;

5— to adorn the book with fine art, including paintings from some of the great museums of the world, as well as with Christmas cards from the Victorian Era and the 20th century, and with popular illustrations from familiar publications such as *The Saturday Evening Post* (whose covers were often graced by the renowned Norman Rockwell), *McCall's*, and *LIFE* magazine, that relate to the Christmas story or tradition and include scenes associated with the Nativity, such as the adoration of the shepherds, or the visit of the three kings, and with images of popular holiday festivities, or figures such as Santa Claus and Rudolph the Red-Nosed Reindeer;

6— to supplement the written text with an exquisite audio collection, including a number of nostalgic and jaunty tunes by some of the finest 20th-century songwriters from the United States.

The seed of inspiration for *THE MILLENNIA COLLECTION: Glorious Christmas Music, Songs, and Carols* and *American Christmas Classics* was probably sown on an early Christmas when I was but one of six hundred boys at St. John's Orphanage in Philadelphia. To this day I have never forgotten the feeling of awe and wonderment I had as a first grader while listening to carols being sung so beautifully by a choir of nuns during my first Midnight Mass.

Nor had I forgotten the popular seasonal songs I heard when kindly Villanova University students took us orphan boys on a shopping tour of downtown Philadelphia. That annual pilgrimage for a Christmas gift, generally an exquisite toy, brought us unimagined joy as we milled around with thousands of busy shoppers, frequently pausing to behold the winter wonderlands so magically displayed in the large storefront windows of such department store giants as John Wanamaker, Gimbels, Lit Brothers, and Strawbridge & Clothier. Our merriment then was of untold, almost mystical, proportion, and the holiday songs that filled the air only added to the rapture of our festive mood. Those memorable occasions have kindled a love for Christmas carols and songs that has remained with me throughout the years.

American Christmas Classics is a legacy that I wish to leave with lovers of Christmas music in America. Perhaps it might be shared by young children and their doting parents or grandparents, or by brothers and sisters, or by close friends who come calling on a holiday visit. Maybe *American Christmas Classics* will cause a harried mother or father lying in bed after a long day to pause long enough to take soothing comfort from the rich heritage of American Christmas music and the nostalgic images associated with it. By chance, the feelings of youth might even well within them as they listen to a holiday tune or view the pages, causing them to recollect the innocence of another time and place when the country seemed far, far less complicated, despite the perils then besetting the world order.

American Christmas Classics seeks to provide a unique approach to the enjoyment of Christmas and its distinctive and wistful music. If only a modicum of that objective is achieved, then this author will indeed have found some satisfaction in contributing to the spirit of a truly wonderful season.

Getting a Holiday Lift
illustration from LIFE,
December 5, 1955
Michael Ramus (b.1917)

American Christmas Classics is the second volume of a series based on information from *THE MILLENNIA COLLECTION: Glorious Christmas Music, Songs, and Carols*, a collection more international in scope. *American Christmas Classics* contains 47 titles of distinguished carols, hymns, and popular holiday songs. Many of the selections are well-known secular Christmas fare from the 20th century. Among the more religious or spiritual titles, the listener will find not only favorite Christmas carols and hymns, but also some of the lesser known variety, from the 18th and 19th centuries.

Birth of the American Carol

Most U.S. contributions to the international Christmas repertoire came after 1843, the year that Charles Dickens' classic holiday story, *A Christmas Carol*, was published. In the United States prior to that time, very few original Christmas carols had been recorded or known to exist. Those heard in the churches of the American colonies in the early 18th century, especially in New England, which was still heavily influenced by the Puritan ethic, were apt to be by Isaac Watts (1674-1748), the noted English poet and composer of hymns.

Given the backdrop of Puritan restrictions on Christmas celebrations, one might readily understand why New England churches favored singing or writing hymns that were more solemn in substance, spurning carols in the process. The Pilgrims, who landed at Plymouth Rock in 1620, even went so far as to shun any observance of Christmas Day by treating it as a normal working day. In 1659 a law passed by the Massachusetts Bay Colony forbade anyone from "observing any such day as Christmas" or that person would be fined five shillings. The "no festival" laws remained on the books until they were finally dropped twenty-two years later. Even after Christmas was fully restored as a holiday in England, it was still severely opposed in New England for many more years. The negative aspects of Puritan restrictions on Christmas celebrations continued well beyond the early 18th century, a major factor in the dearth of quality American carols at the time.

Another reason for the early lack of American carols was that most colonial composers were less exposed to sophisticated music and were less educated, by and large, than their English counterparts, although their songs of the people were readily understood. The lyrics and tunes coming from American native schools were likely to be less refined in nature, although not necessarily lacking in originality. Since instrumental music was little cultivated in New England churches, a condition resulting from Puritan disdain for it or because many churches could not afford an organ, original American hymn compositions were very few.

Some original carol compositions from New England resulted from the efforts of William Billings (1746-1800), a self-taught music teacher and tanner by trade.

Facing page:
Street Scene, Christmas Morn, *1892*
Childe Hassam (1859-1935)
Smith College Museum of Art

Billings made his mark during the Revolutionary War era with a fiercely independent, almost eccentric, style that was based on a musical idiom of the country parish church that was commonplace in 18th century England. Typical of his New England heritage, his compositions were more Pentecostal than joyous, such as his "The Shepherd's Carol", and his musical style, to some degree, would be imitated a century later by Charles Ives (1874-1954), one of America's first internationally acclaimed composers. Ives wrote a number of hymns in his own youth, contributing to the Christmas repertoire with his "A Christmas Carol".

In other parts of the country during the period spanning the 17th to mid-19th centuries, settlers sang carols, mostly from Europe, in their native tongues. The colonies in the South celebrated Christmas in aristocratic fashion. Latin tunes and English carols were enjoyed by Catholic churchgoers in Maryland and other Catholic enclaves in the Mid-Atlantic states. Vernacular carols and Latin hymns could be heard in the vast territories of the country that were once dominated by Spain, a former colonial power. The French celebrated in Louisiana, Missouri, Illinois, and in parts of what was once known as the Northwest Territories. The Episcopalians celebrated in Virginia, and the Moravians in parts of Pennsylvania and North Carolina. In New York the influence of the Dutch was especially strong, and to a large degree their customs, as well as those of the Germans and other Europeans, would be embraced by Americans.

An Hymn for Christmas (words taken from Isaac Watts hymn)
First hymn from William Billings "Eight Christmas Pieces", 1770

Dickens' U.S. contemporary Washington Irving (1783-1859), who loved English customs and traditions, strove to influence the American public to partake of English Christmas celebrations. But Americans, because of their disdain of anything associated with the English after the end of the Revolutionary War, were more likely to adopt Christmas customs brought to America by Dutch explorers. Even Irving had prominently mentioned "Sinta Klaes", the venerable Dutch figure of St. Nicholas, six times in his work *The Knickerbocker History of New York*.

The advocacy of Washington Irving, coupled with the great success Charles Dickens' holiday classic enjoyed in the United States, coincided with the onset of the Victorian Era and helped to open the floodgates for significant carol contributions by American composers. Many of these carols were poems that would later be set to music. In 1849 Edmund H. Sears (1810-1876), a clergyman, wrote the poem "It Came Upon the Midnight Clear". James S. Pierpont (1822-1893) wrote the words and music for "Jingle Bells", the first and most famous of American secular carols, in 1857. In the same year John H. Hopkins (1820-1891) composed "We Three Kings of Orient Are". Another poem made famous as a carol

Christmas Waits in England
engraving from 1875 edition of
"The Sketch Book"

was "O Little Town of Bethlehem", written by the Rev. Phillips Brooks (1835-1893) in 1868 for his Sunday school children in Philadelphia. "Away in a Manger", an important carol hymn published in 1885, was actually an anonymous composition that for years had been erroneously attributed to Martin Luther. The rightful composer of the music was discovered to be James Murray (1841-1905), an American compiler of song books. These original American carols helped to end a two-hundred-year drought of quality English-language carols.

Some of our most heartfelt folk carols came from black slaves and rural people, including a majority of the carols composed in the United States up to the post-Civil War and late-19th century period. Most likely created between the mid-18th and mid-19th centuries, these folk carols were essentially religious or spiritual in nature, outnumbering secular carols and songs by a 5:1 ratio, according to statistics based on information from *Christmas Carols: A Reference Guide,* by William Studwell. Approximately 60% of American carols cited in Studwell's guide are described as anonymous contributions of black slaves or folks from Appalachia.

This lack of attribution is understandable because although writers took note of black slaves and their singing, few commented on the songs in any detail. "Go Tell It on the Mountain", probably one of the more recent 19th century spiritual compositions, and "Mary Had a Baby", were carols whose simple theme and un-pretentious lyrics represented the purest designs of St. Francis Assisi, a saintly monk who in 1223 encouraged the enactment of Christ's humble birth in an open air setting. These carols swelled from the deepest recesses of an enslaved people's collective soul to honor their Lord Jesus, to whom they prayed to help them out of their terrible bondage.

By the close of the 19th century some Christmas customs and carol singing had become thoroughly entrenched tradition. Santa Claus was by then a favorite Christmas figure in the United States as a result of the publication of Clement Moore's 1822 poem, *A Visit from St. Nicholas*, or *'Twas the Night Before Christmas*. In both England and the United States it was customary for carols to be sung, not only in the churches, but also by groups of carolers who gathered outside the houses of friends or strangers. The decoration of Christmas trees was common-place in the English-speaking world, as well as other Christian countries, of the

The Christmas Tree
*19th century watercolor and
gouache, American School
The Museum of the City of
New York*

Victorian Age. German tree ornaments were the rage and in great demand.

With the carol having reclaimed its rightful place in the hearts of English-speaking people everywhere and the shadows cast by Puritanism finally receding, the carol was in a robust state of health, and the 20th century witnessed its continued growth and the rise of American secular holiday songs.

20th-Century Holiday Songs By far the largest contributor of songs and carols to the 20th-century portion of *THE MILLENNIA COLLECTION: Glorious Christmas Music, Songs and Carols,* and the primary focus of *American Christmas Classics*, is the United States. A major reason for this reality was the early dominance of American industry in creating and manufacturing audio products. The 1877 invention of the phonograph, and subsequent technological improvements to it in the late 1890s and early 1900s by pioneer recording companies, including Columbia Phonograph and Victor Company, contributed significantly to a whole new way of promoting popular songs. At that time the sale of sheet mu-

Santa with His Reindeer
1912 book illustration
Mary Cowles
(active 1980-1905)

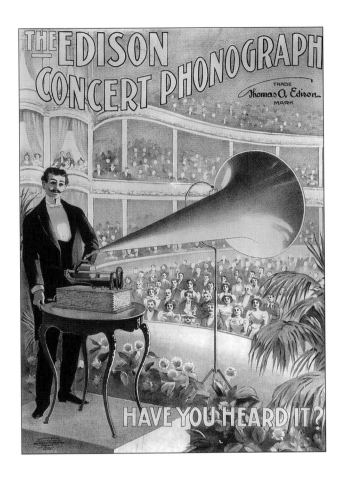

The Edison Concert
Phonograph
1888 U.S. Printing Co. poster

sic was the best gauge for determining what type of music ordinary people liked.

During the period from 1900 to 1920, well-known American and European singers and musicians began to record Christmas songs and carols for the first time. The development of 33 rpm long-playing and 45 rpm single records by mid-century, plus the evolution of electronic microprocessor technologies leading to the development of the audio cassette and then the compact disc, all helped to sustain this trend.

These audio technologies enabled more people to appreciate the wide range of musical styles, giving impetus to those who wanted to study music or had an appetite for serious or casual composition. The speed of modern communication, especially radio, which had nurtured and secured the loyalty of large audiences for music, heightened awareness of the originality of all types of music, not only from around the country but also from around the globe.

Radio audiences enjoyed neoclassic compositions and other forms of modern music, such as *musique concrete*, which drew on the everyday sounds of street life. The growth of modern music was aided by American record companies, whose early experience and expertise in shrewdly marketing audio music, including tra-

Old St. Nick
cover of Country Gentleman,
December 1925
N.C. Wyeth (1882-1945)

ditional Christmas carols sung by well-known individuals and groups, helped to extend their influence on 20th-century music. This influence was exerted over the radio and in talking movie parlors of the late 1920s, which proved a further boon for merchandising records.

Until the late 1940s and early 1950s radio especially was king. At that time it did not have to compete with television. People from all walks of life listened to radio programs for their entertainment, and they enjoyed the singing of such stars as Kate Smith, Bing Crosby, the Andrews Sisters, Nat "King" Cole, and Perry Como, and the music of Glenn Miller, the Dorsey Brothers, and Guy Lombardo. The introduction of new songs by these radio stars could easily catapult them to successful runs on national sales charts. Such was the case for the song "Santa Claus Is Comin' to Town" when Eddie Cantor first introduced it in 1934 on his popular radio show. "Winter Wonderland" became a hit the same year when Guy Lombardo and his Royal Canadians recorded it. The Andrews Sisters and Perry Como brought it to the public's attention again in 1946 with separate recordings, the year when Nat "King" Cole first launched the ever popular "The Christmas Song". Many of these new holiday songs from the United States that became commercial winners were secular in nature.

"White Christmas" and World War II   Besides the tremendous impact of radio, other events helped to spur the writing of secular holiday songs. One was the phenomenal success of Irving Berlin's "White Christmas". Written in 1940, though not available to the public until the release of the movie *Holiday Inn* two years later, "White Christmas" went on to become one of the best-selling single records of all time. Another pivotal influence was World War II and its aftermath. As the war in the Pacific and across the European continent raged on, the sentimental strains of "White Christmas" and other wonderful holiday songs, including "I'll Be Home for Christmas" and "Have Yourself a Merry Little Christmas", became popular with American soldiers and sailors. These songs reminded

Freedom from Want
cover of The Saturday
Evening Post, *March 6, 1943*
Norman Rockwell (1894-1978)

America's men and women of their families and being nestled at home for the Christmas holidays. In their own unique way they gave expression to a profound sentimentality that was uplifting and morale boosting, and they reflected the values of a united, hard-working people who served the interests of family and country by strongly supporting the American war effort in what they believed was the cause of righteousness.

When the hostilities of World War II finally ended in 1945, Americans and people from around the globe, especially those from nations heavily affected by the terrible conflict, celebrated the good news. But because it had been spared the great devastation of its continental territory and economic industries, the United States was better equipped to take advantage of the fruits of victory. One way in which this good fortune manifested itself was in the mostly upbeat and charming quality of holiday songs. From 1940 to 1954, sixteen of the American secular Christmas songs contained in this collection, most of them quite popular, were published. Two of them, "There Is No Christmas Like a Home Christmas" and "Christmas Eve in My Home Town", were released while another foreign war involving American troops was being waged. The Korean War evoked some of the same holiday nostalgia and passion as World War II. Of these sixteen songs, four were produced in 1950 alone!

The Wrong Shall Fail, the Right Prevail
illustration from 1942 carol songbook

The Wrong Shall Fail, the Right Prevail

1940 - *White Christmas*
1943 - *I'll Be Home for Christmas*
1944 - *Have Yourself a Merry Little Christmas*
1945 - *Let It Snow! Let It Snow! Let It Snow!*
1946 - *The Christmas Song*
1947 - *Here Comes Santa Claus*
1948 - *Blue Christmas*
1948 - *Sleigh Ride*
1949 - *Rudolph the Red-Nosed Reindeer*
1950 - *Christmas in Killarney*
1950 - *Frosty the Snow Man*
1950 - *It's Beginning to Look Like Christmas*
1950 - *There Is No Christmas Like a Home Christmas*
1951 - *Christmas Eve in My Home Town*
1951 - *Silver Bells*
1954 - *The Christmas Waltz*

The period from 1934 to 1958 could rightfully be called "The Golden Age" of American secular holiday songs. That was not surprising since the 20th century witnessed the almost total secularization of all the arts, including music. In

The Joyous Sounds of
Christmas
illustration from LIFE,
December 11, 1944

their own fashion many of these wonderful secular tunes possessed tender lyrics of a quality that helped to engage the human spirit, representing the many moods of Christmas—bright, cheerful, nostalgic, and on occasion, even sad.

Although Christmas is primarily a religious holiday celebrated by Christians throughout the world, the addition of tuneful secular songs over the centuries has added much to the wonderful mix of music. In America during the 20th century, Jewish songwriters and composers were major contributors of holiday songs, perhaps because the religious holiday of *Hanukkah* occurs at about the same time as Christmas, or maybe just because Americans simply loved their sentimental or snappy lyrics and tunes. Irving Berlin gave us "White Christmas". Johnny Marks wrote the lyrics and music to the quickly popular "Rudolph the Red-Nosed Reindeer", the first successful Christmas character from America since Clement Moore's introduction of Santa Claus in 1822. In addition, he composed a variant tune for "I Heard the Bells on Christmas Day", a song based on the Henry Wadsworth Longfellow poem *Christmas Bells*, and "Rockin' Around the Christmas Tree", a cheery song reflective of the rock-and-roll era. Sammy Cahn and Jule Styne collaborated on the delightfully charming "Let It Snow! Let It Snow! Let It Snow!". Nine years later they wrote "The ChristmasWaltz" for Frank Sinatra, perhaps the greatest American entertainer of the 20th century. Mel Torme, with the able support of his good friend Robert Wells, gave us the warm tune and lyrics for "The Christmas Song". Carl Sigman penned the words for "There Is No Christmas Like a Home Christmas".

The contributions of 20th-century American Jewish songwriters in the secular realm has been significant, just as the authorship of melodic *alleluias* sung by their forbears of several millennia ago, the cantors in the ancient synagogue, paved the way in the spiritual realm of Christian music at the outset of Christianity. Overall, the contributions of many members of the American songwriting community helped to make the Christmas season all the more delightful.

20th-Century Carols and Hymns   On the other side of the musical ledger, the United States continued to make serious contributions to the religious music repertoire. From 1933 to 1966, nine of the carols or hymns collected in this volume were written or discovered. Their number is smaller, compared with the number of secular songs composed during a similar period because 1) the fantastic commercial success of "White Christmas" encouraged a slew of other composers to emulate Irving Berlin, and 2) the ushering in of the rock-and-roll era around 1954 helped to expand American dominance of pop culture on the world scene. The Christmas songs "Jingle Bell Rock" and "Rockin' Around the Christmas Tree" were early entries of this new musical style.

Nevertheless, American folk carols and hymns of the 20th century continue this country's heritage of quality religious compositions, despite the growing popularity and publication of secular music. These religious Christmas compositions are infused with simple love and joy. The carols of Wihla Hutson and Alfred Burt and his father, the Rev. Bates G. Burt, are golden nuggets. "The Star Carol", "Some Children See Him", and "Caroling, Caroling" replicate the earnest simplicity of early English carols from the 14th and 15th centuries. "Do You Hear What I Hear?" relates with gentle beauty the coming of a newborn King. "The Little Drummer Boy" may be the finest carol coming from the United States in the last fifty years, its humble lyrics reflecting the supreme nobility of hope and faith. "Cowboy Carol" emerges triumphantly from the rugged terrain and the wide open spaces of the American Southwest where the joy of a new world beginning shines like a wondrous brilliant star.

Some of the most humble and unforgettable religious compositions came from the hand of John Jacob Niles, a pre-eminent folklorist, who in the 1930s discovered "I Wonder As I Wander" and "Jesus, Jesus, Rest Your Head". Both of these carols represented the heartfelt entreaties of simple people honoring the birth of Christ.

The Christmas Calendar The carols and hymns compiled in this volume are some of America's finest contributions to both the international and

Nativity Greetings, *c.1938*
American Christmas card
Free Library of Philadelphia

The Cathedral of Christmas
cover of The Saturday
Evening Post
December 3, 1949
John Falter (1910-1982)

Christmas repertoire, and they are helpful reminders of the overall relevance of Christmas. Not only do such carols reflect religious inclinations, but they also serve as friendly reminders of the dates on the calendar when Christmas and other religious feasts were honored. Because the Christmas holidays in the United States begin on Thanksgiving Day and end on Christmas Day evening, as indicated by the playing of Christmas and holiday music in public places or over the airwaves, the American Christmas calendar hardly corresponds with the traditional feast days honored by the music and songs of the ages. Many carols, especially those from the British Isles, were written for dates after Christmas Day. For example, carols were written to honor St. Stephen's Day (December 26th), the Feast of the Holy Innocents (December 28th), New Year's Eve (December 31st), New Year's Day, or the Circumcision of Our Lord (January 1st), and the Epiphany, or Visit of the Magi (January 6th), and Candlemas (February 2nd). For centuries in Europe and the British Isles, Candlemas represented the official close of the Church calendar's Christmas season.

Besides commemorating the Nativity, carols retold the stories of the Annunciation, the Visitation of the Virgin Mary, and other important events of the Christian Church. The verses of the old English secular carol "The Twelve Days of Christmas" start with Christmas Day as the first of the twelve days, and they conclude with January 6th, also known as the Twelfth Night. A suggestion for Americans: Why not lift the moratorium on Christmas music after December 25th?

Considering how so much emphasis is placed on the less important aspects of Christmas, particularly the ever-increasing commercialization of this special time of year, is it any wonder that our Christmas calendar has become skewed? Or that the more meaningful themes of the season have become overshadowed? This musing is certainly not new. It has been registered as a complaint with each new generation, and more so after we have exhausted ourselves, yet again, from the perfunctory shopping and buying of another Christmas season. In such a frantic flow, we hardly pause long enough to recognize and enjoy our seasonal music, songs, or carols—the very same ones that are played continuously, and ironically, on many of our shopping rounds.

Perhaps one way for us to enjoy the essential spirit of our traditional Christmas is to slow down and take stock of our wonderful blessings, even though we may feel little inclination to unwind and appreciate them. Hence, another reason behind the creation of *American Christmas Classics* is to offer it as a remedy for soothing the soul and bringing good cheer to a ladened heart.

So listen up! Look for "a star in the sky or a bird on the wing." Sing a carol whose central beauty elevates the human condition. And when you come down from those soaring heights, treat yourself and your family and friends to a lovely sleigh ride and hear the ring-ting-tingling too!

Songs & Carols Collection

The Trombone Choir in the
Cupola of the Moravian
Church in Bethlehem
*mural from State Capitol of
Pennsylvania*
William Brantley Van Ingen
(1858-1955)

1 ❋ *Away in a Manger*

Recording Artist—
Tanya Tucker

Words—
Anonymous 18th- to 19th-century American folk

Music—
James Ramsey Murray (1841-1905), American composer and compiler of music

A well-known carol hymn of obscure origins, "Away in a Manger" may have been written by a member of the German Lutheran colony in Pennsylvania during the late 19th century. The anonymous words for the first two stanzas originally appeared in 1885 in the *Little Children's Book for Schools and Families*, a publication of the Evangelical Lutheran Church in North America. The source of the words may have been an 1883 poem commemorating the 400th anniversary of the birth of Martin Luther. Although many modern hymnals attribute the lyrics of the third stanza to John T. McFarland (1851-1913), a member of the American Lutheran Board of Sunday Schools, it is believed he had merely made reference to it. Instead, the third stanza, which first appeared in an 1892 Louisville, Kentucky, Lutheran Church collection titled *Gabriel's Vineyard Songs*, was probably the contribution of another anonymous author. This lyrical addition strengthens the inherent tenderness of this renowned American carol hymn.

The words and music of this tender hymn were once also thought to have been composed by Martin Luther (1483-1546), the great German religious reformer, and it was often referred to as "Luther's Cradle Hymn". However, by the 1940s it was proven conclusively that the music had actually been composed by James Ramsey Murray, supposedly the same person who perpetrated the myth of "Luther's Cradle Hymn". Murray, who might also have used the pseudonym of Mueller, a name totally untraceable yet found in association with "Away in a Manger" in many hymnals, probably allowed his fanciful imagination to get the better of him, certainly not the first time that someone got enthusiastic about the Christmas experience, and his lullaby was included in an 1887 Cincinnati collection called *Dainty Songs for Lads and Lasses*. Since then, at least forty-one known tunes have been associated with the carol, including those of American composers Jonathan E. Spilman (1812-1896) and William J. Kirkpatrick (1838-1921). The familiar musical settings of Spilman and Kirkpatrick, however, are more likely to be heard in England. Murray's tune, generally sung in a southern Baptist style, such as by Tanya Tucker (b.1958), is standard in the United States.

During the late 19th century, Pennsylvania Germans and Moravians were noted for several unique Christmas customs. They celebrated the humble beginnings of the Christ Child by employing a Christmas decoration called a putz (from the German word "putzen" meaning "to adorn"), for the manger scene. The Moravians, furthermore, may even have played the music for "Away in a Manger" in trombone choirs that were known to perform from church belfries in Bethlehem, Nazareth, and other Pennsylvania towns with Moravian congregations.

Bethlehem, the site of the first Moravian church built in eastern Pennsylvania, was so named on Christmas Eve in 1742 when construction of the church was completed. That special night settlers sang in one room of the new structure while cows mooed in the other half, which was a stable. The scene so moved the congregation, reminding them of events surrounding the birth of the Christ Child in another small town eighteen-hundred years earlier, that they christened their settlement Bethlehem.

Away in a manger, no crib for a bed,
The little Lord Jesus laid down His sweet Head.
The stars in the bright sky looked down where He Lay,
The little Lord Jesus asleep on the hay.

The cattle are lowing, the Baby awakes,
But little Lord Jesus no crying He makes.
I love Thee, Lord Jesus, look down from the sky,
And stay by my cradle till morning is nigh.

Be near me, Lord Jesus, I ask Thee to stay
Close by me forever and love me I pray.
Bless all the dear children in Thy tender care,
And take us to heaven to live with Thee There.

Martin Luther and His Family at Wittenberg, Christmas Eve, 1536
engraving by James Bannister (1821-1901)

Recording Artist—
James McCracken

Words & Music—
William H. Neidlinger
(1863-1924),
American composer,
organist, and conductor

The 1880s and 1890s represented the Victorian era at its height, a time when Christmas card creations blossomed as a distinct art form. In America such art was encouraged through prize-awarding competitions sponsored by greeting card publishers, especially by Louis Prang (1824-1909), a German immigrant and "Father of the American Christmas Card", who perfected a lithographic process to inexpensively produce colored pictures. English and American Christmas cards, as well as fine art paintings, often depicted children, especially young girls, as angels clothed in white. Other familiar motifs associated with this illustrative art form

Angel, 1889
Abbott Handerson Thayer
(1849-1921)
National Museum of American
Art, Smithsonian Institution

included people transported by horse carriage or sleigh over snowbound roads and hills, in addition to typical scenes related to the Nativity.

It was during this era, in 1890 to be precise, that William Neidlinger composed "The Birthday of a King". Neidlinger, besides being an accomplished musician and composer of a number of comic operas and songs, was a top-notch voice teacher who was known in Europe and America. He also was involved with the education of retarded children, who at that time were defined as "subnormal". Intended to be sung as a solo, this Victorian composition quite aptly describes the humble mood inspired by the manger scene.

In a little village of Bethlehem,
There lay a Child one day,
And the sky was bright with a holy light
O'er the place where Jesus lay:

    REFRAIN:
    Alleluia! O how the angels sang,
    Alleluia! how it rang;
    And the sky was bright with a holy light
    'Twas the birthday of a King.

'Twas the humble birthplace,
But oh! how much God gave to us that day,
From the manger bed, what a path has led
What a perfect holy way:
    REFRAIN:

Birthday of a King
*1898 American Christmas Card
from Louis Prang Co.
National Museum of American
History, Smithsonian Institution*

Recording Artist—
Tammy Wynette

Words & Music—
Billy Hayes (b.1906),
American songwriter
and guitarist;
Jay W. Johnson
(1903-1986),
American songwriter and
entertainer

"Blue Christmas" is an American secular Christmas song with a strong country flavor. It was composed by Billy Hayes and Jay W. Johnson, the latter having spent 70 years in show business, including radio and television where he was involved with over 1,000 shows and their syndication. First published in 1948, "Blue Christmas" was released as a recording during the 1949 Christmas season by the well-known big band leader, Russ Morgan (1904-1969). Hugo Winterholter (1909-1973), another noted big band leader, and Ernest Tubb (1914-1984), a popular country singer, followed up in 1950 with their respective recordings. Elvis Presley (1935-1977), an enormously popular American rock-and-roll star, helped to make "Blue Christmas" a big hit in the 1960s, and since then a number of country recording artists have added their interpretations.

Tammy Wynette (1943-1998), a wonderful country singer whose own life in some respects epitomized personal misfortune and heartache, perfectly enunciates the song's theme of lost and unrequited love. Quite unusual for Christmas because it contrasts starkly with the joy and merriment often associated with the season, the song captures the loneliness of a stranger.

I'll have a blue Christmas without you;
I'll be so blue thinking about you.
Decorations of red on a green Christmas tree
Won't mean a thing if you're not here with me.

I'll have a blue Christmas, that's certain;
And when that blue heartache starts hurtin',
You'll be doin' all right with your Christmas of white
But I'll have a blue, blue Christmas.

Stranger in Town
Melvin C. Warren (1920-1995)
Private Collection

4 ✤ *Carol, Brothers, Carol*

Recording Artists—
Fred Waring &
The Pennsylvanians

Words & Music—
William Augustus
Muhlenberg (1796-1877),
American clergyman,
composer, and music
compiler

Written sometime during the 19th century, "Carol, Brothers, Carol" is a fine example of a carol conveying a genuine sense of warmth and good feeling. The creator of the words and original music, William Augustus Muhlenberg, was an eminent Episcopalian clergyman who compiled several church tune books and wrote church poetry. He even wrote a hymn commemorating President Abraham Lincoln for officially proclaiming on October 3, 1863, during the height of the Civil War, a day of Thanksgiving for the nation. Lincoln had set aside the fourth Thursday of each November as "a day of thanksgiving and praise to our beneficent Father who dwelleth in the heavens". Lincoln's decision was highly influenced by Sarah Josepha Hale (1788-1879), editor of *Godey's Lady's Book*, a Philadelphia publication, and author of the famous nursery rhyme "Mary Had a Little Lamb".

By the end of the Civil War, however, it was difficult for many to celebrate Thanksgiving in a festive fashion. Food was awfully scarce. Many people with little food would donate some of it to others who had nothing to eat. What made matters worse were the high prices. A turkey could cost as much as $100. The price of candy was $8.00 a pound. From the depths of such grief and turmoil, however, hope sprang eternal, and eventually Thanksgiving would become one of the nation's highly anticipated holidays.

William Augustus Muhlenberg was also a great grandson of Henry Melchior Muhlenberg (1711-1787), a distinguished German Lutheran sent to America by his superiors to help organize the Lutheran settlements, which at the time were quite fragmented. Henry Melchior Muhlenberg was so successful in his mission that he is considered the Patriarch of American Lutheranism. He is buried in Trappe, Pennsylvania.

Interestingly, that area of the nation was heavily settled by Germans and is often mistakenly referred to as "Pennsylvania Dutch country", the word "Dutch" having been confused with the word "Deutsch", meaning "German". Another misadventure with the German language occurs in Christmas lore. "Christkindl", the German term for the Christ Child, was thought to be Kriss Kringle, who would become a popular holiday figure. Although unintended, these misnomers have a good natured appeal and are now permanent fixtures in the American lexicon.

The contemporary musical setting of "Carol, Brothers, Carol" is the work of Roy Ringwald (b.1910), a composer and songwriter who devised a number of arrangements over the years for Fred Waring (1900-1984), an American conductor, music publisher, and songwriter. There is little doubt that his 20th-century embellishment of Muhlenberg's light lyrics captures the true spirit of fellowship and Christmas song writing of the mid-19th century.

REFRAIN:
Carol, brothers, carol,
Carol joyfully,
Carol the glad tidings,
Carol merrily!
And pray a gladsome Christmas
For all good Christian men,
Carol, brothers, carol,
Christmas time again.

Carol, but with gladness
Not in songs of earth;
On the Saviour's birthday
Hallow'd be our mirth.
While the merry season
Fills us all with glee,
We'll be keeping Christmas
His Nativity.
    REFRAIN:

Home to Thanksgiving,
1867 "Currier & Ives"
color lithograph
The Museum of the City
of New York

Hearing angel music,
Discord sure must cease;
Who dare hate his brother
On this day of peace?
While the heav'ns are telling
To mankind goodwill,
Only love and kindness
Ev'ry thought fulfill.
    REFRAIN:

Let our hearts, responding
To the angel band,
With the festal sunshine
Bright in ev'ry land:
Word and deed and prayer
Speak the grateful sound,
Telling "Merry Christmas"
All the world around.
    REFRAIN:

5   *Carol of the Bells*

Other Titles—
Ukrainian Christmas Carol;
Shchedryk

Recording Artists—
Mormon Tabernacle Choir/
The Columbia Symphony
Orchestra;
Jerold Ottley, director

Words—
Peter J . Wilhousky
(1902-1978),
American music teacher
and composer

Music—
Mykola Dmytrovych
Leontovych (1877-1921),
Ukrainian composer

This is an exceptionally joyous carol that is based on "Shchedryk", a 1916 arrangement of a traditional "shchedrivka" ritual song by Mykola Leontovych, a composer of liturgical music and choral miniatures based on Ukrainian folk songs. Three years later, after Ukraine gained independence as a result of World War I, the newly-formed government sent the Ukrainian National Choir around the world to act as its goodwill ambassador. Under the direction of renowned conductor Oleksander Koshets (1875-1944), the choir toured for five years singing a repertoire of Ukrainian songs, including "Shchedryk" by Leontovych. European and American audiences marveled at this fascinating composition. Peter J. Wilhousky, an American school teacher of Ukrainian ancestry, was so impressed by it that he wrote the English lyrics and had them published in 1936 under the new title "Carol of the Bells". Although Wilhousky's lyrics are not a translation of the Ukrainian words, they still retain the joyous spirit of "Shchedryk" as it was transformed from a New Year's composition to a Christmas carol.

"Shchedrivka" or "Shchedryk" (from "shchedre" or generous), a Ukrainian deity of bounty, was represented in the original form as a female bird. Winged

deities appeared in two types of pre-Christian ritual songs sung during the holiday season: 1) "Koliadky", describing the creation of the world (doves)— as well as the later-derived Christian "koliady", or Christmas carols celebrating the birth of Christ (angels); and 2) "Shchedrivky", hopeful songs of the New Year, sung by carolers as incantations mimicking rhythmic bird sounds to bring in a bountiful year. It was these rhythmic bird sounds that Wilhousky interpreted as bells in his English text.

From ancient pagan times to the early 18th century, "Shchedryk" was actually sung in the month of March, then considered the New Year on the Ukrainian calendar (but since moved to January). It relates how a swallow returns in early Spring and sings to a farmer, calling upon him to enjoy the rich blessings of crops and livestock, or his bounty, thus posing a picture quite different from the snow-filled village scenes one might expect of a wintry New Year's Eve in Ukraine. As part of the festivities, married women, maidens, and children ("shchedrivka chirpers") began their caroling on New Year's Eve, during the Bountiful Dinner (Shchedra Vechera), and they continued their singing of well-wishing songs through the whole season.

The theme of bounty was also associated with the Holy Supper, or Sviata Vechera, a central tradition of Christmas Eve. On that night, Ukrainian families celebrated their spiritual bounty with a feast consisting of twelve foods. As a reminder of the manger of the Nativity, dishes are placed on a table covered with embroidered cloth and strewn with hay. The feast begins when the children of the family have sighted the first evening star in the eastern sky, symbolizing the Star of Bethlehem that once guided the journey of the Three Wise Men. But in a farmer's home the feast begins only after a sheaf of wheat (Didukh), inhabited by the spirits of the ancestors, has been brought into the house. After the Christmas Eve feast, the Ukrainian household celebrates by singing Koliady or joining caroling groups to visit neighbors' homes.

The story behind "Carol of the Bells" and how it was converted from "Shchedryk", a Ukrainian New Year's ritual song of ancient pagan origin, to an American Christmas carol is quite an amazing one. What makes it an even more memorable composition, especially as it is performed by the Mormon Tabernacle Choir and instrumental accompaniment, is the incorporation of steady tintinnabulation, or the ringing of bells. Whether you're out on a carol round, or sipping hot cider with oatmeal cookies, the wonderful texture of "Carol of the Bells" puts it on the "must list" of songs to be enjoyed during this favorite holiday season.

Village in Winter, *1891*
Piotr Levchenko (1859-1917),
Ukrainian National Art
Museum, Kiev

Based on tune from this
UKRAINIAN song:

Щедрик, щедрик, щедрівочка,
Прилетіла ластівочка,
Стала собі щебетати,
Господаря викликати:
"Вийди, вийди, господарю,
Подивися на кошару,
Там овечки покотились,
А ягнички народились.
В тебе товар ввесь хороший, —
Будеш мати мірку грошей.
Хоч не гроші, то полова,
В тебе жінка чорноброва."
Щедрик, щедрик, щедрівочка,
Прилетіла ластівочка.

Christmas Chimes
*Early 20th-century print
reproduction after a painting
by Edwin Blashfield
(1848-1936)*

ENGLISH

Hark! how the bells,
Sweet silver bells,
All seem to say.
"Throw cares away."
Christmas is here,
Bringing good cheer
To young and old,
Meek and the bold
Ding, dong, ding, dong,
That is their song
With joyful ring,
All caroling.
One seems to hear
Words of good cheer
From ev'rywhere
Filling the air;
O, how they pound,
Raising the sound
O'er hill and dale,
Telling their tale.
Gaily they ring
While people sing
Songs of good cheer,
Christmas is here!
Merry, merry, merry, merry
Christmas,
Merry, merry, merry, merry
Christmas,
On, on they send,
On without end,
Their joyful tone
To ev'ry home.
Ding, dong, ding, dong.

(Repeat the above)

UKRAINIAN *(in English phonetics)*:	ENGLISH translation by Lavrentia Turkewicz (b.1960):
Shchedryk, shchedryk, shchedrivochka,	Generous Goddess, Generous Goddess,
Pryletila lastivochka,	The swallow has flown in.
Stala sobi shchebetaty,	She started chirping,
Hospodaria vyklykaty:	Calling out the master of the house.
"Vyjdy, vyjdy, hospodariu,	"Come out, come out, master,
Podyvysja na kosharu,	Look at your hurdling:
Tam ovechky pokotylys',	The lambs are brought forth,
A jahnychky narodylys',	And the ewes are born.
V tebe tovar ves' khoroshyi,	You have good livestock
Budesh maty mirku hroshei.	For which you will beget good money.
Khoch ne hroshi, to polova,	If not money, you get chaff,
V tebe zhinka chornobrova."	But you still have a black-browed wife."

A fine 20-century American carol, "Caroling, Caroling" was first published the year Alfred Burt died at the young age of thirty-three. It was written by Wihla Hutson, a close friend of Alfred Burt and an organist of fifty years for four different churches, including All Saints Church of Pontiac, Michigan. This is the same church where the Rev. Bates G. Burt (1878-1948), the father of Alfred, who was the composer of the music for "Caroling, Caroling", served as Rector for twenty-five years.

Rev. Bates Burt , a devoted father, loved music almost as much as he loved

Recording Artists—
Fred Waring &
The Pennsylvanians

Words—
Wihla Hutson (b.1901),
American church organist
and songwriter

Music—
Alfred S. Burt (1920-1954),
American composer and
jazz trumpeter

Carolers, illustration from Ideals Magazine, *December 1953*

his family. In 1926 he had an idea about writing a carol, one which would sing about his feelings of Christmas, and he and his wife would send it to their friends as a Christmas card. So began this family custom, and year after year their many friends looked forward to receiving these charming cards from the Burt family. Eventually their own three children and grandchildren were added to the Christmas card list.

When Alfred, the youngest child, had finished college with a music degree, the Rev. Burt said, "I think the time has come for me to turn over to you the writing of the music for the annual carol, and I will continue to write the words." Beginning in 1941, the carols came from father and son—the music reflecting the true spirit of Christmas. After 1948 when the Rev. Burt died, his son and Wihla Hutson, an old family friend who had spent many Christmases with the Burt family, continued the lovely practice of composing annual Christmas carols until Alfred's own death.

Despite their passing, the wonderful legacy of the Burts, as well as the contributions of Wihla Hutson, is now part of the American carol repertoire. "Caroling, Caroling", perhaps the last collaboration of Hutson and the younger Burt, represents the traditional good feelings associated with the Burt family compositions. Notice how its simple lyrics and carefree lilt entices us to sing along while Christmas bells are ringing.

Caroling, caroling, now we go;
Christmas bells are ringing!
Caroling, caroling, thru the snow;
Christmas bells are ringing!
Joyous voices sweet and clear,
Sing the sad of heart to cheer.
Ding, dong, ding, dong,
Christmas bells are ringing!

Caroling, caroling, thru the town;
Christmas bells are ringing!
Caroling, caroling, up and down;
Christmas bells are ringing!
Mark ye well the song we sing,
Gladsome tidings now we bring.
Ding, dong, ding, dong,
Christmas bells are ringing!

7 ⁂ A Christmas Carol

Recording Artists—
The Western Wind Singers

Words—
Anonymous 19th-century
American folk

Music—
Charles Ives (1874-1954),
American composer

This modern and interesting American carol was first published in 1935 although it was most likely composed much earlier, perhaps during the 1890s, when Charles Ives was a student at Yale University. Ives was regarded in international music circles as one of the first distinctively great American composers, an honor that could as easily have been bestowed on William Billings (1746-1800), a tanner by trade and a composer during the American Revolutionary War era. Just as Billings was opposed to academic canons about music composing, so, too, was Ives. Ives believed in the use of discordant notes (a common trait of today's popular music), which went against the musical conventions of his time. Such musical innovation by Ives, once exploited by Billings himself, would eventually be copied by his European peers of the early to mid-20th century.

Ives began his music career early in life, serving as an organist at the age of

Angels Beneath the Tall Tree
book illustration, 1912
Florence Edith Storer
(active 1900-1915)

thirteen when he learned by heart a number of hymns that he cherished. "A Christmas Carol", a sacred carol composition that uses the slow-rocking harmony of a lullaby, might have come to him as an inspiration during his days performing on the church organ.

On Earth Peace Among Men
of Good Will
*late 19th century American
Christmas card
Thomas Moran (1837-1926)
National Museum of American
History, Smithsonian Institution*

Little star of Bethlehem!
Do we see thee now?
Do we see thee shining
O'er the tall trees?
Little Child of Bethlehem!
Do we hear thee in our hearts?
Hear the angels singing:
"Peace on earth, good will to men! *Noel!*"

O'er the cradle of a King,
Hear the angels sing:
"In excelsis gloria, gloria!"
From his father's home on high,
Lo! for us He came to die;
Hear the angels sing:
"Venite adoremus Dominum."

Translations:
In excelsis gloria, gloria -
Glory in the highest, glory
Venite adoremus Dominum -
O come, let us adore him, the Lord

8 ❈ *Christmas Eve in My Home Town*

Recording Artist—
Kate Smith;
Arranged & conducted by
Peter Matz

Words & Music—
Stan Zabka (b.1924),
American songwriter
Don Upton (1925-1978),
American songwriter

Although the period from 1930 to 1950 was negatively affected by the Great Depression and World War II and its immediate aftermath, it was also a time when radio emerged as a large influence on popular culture. Amid the hardships of people's everyday lives, radio provided countless millions of people around the world with welcome relief by carrying the sounds of popular vocal groups and soloists. In the United States one of the most popular vocalists of the period was Kate Smith (1909-1986). Her rousing rendition of "God Bless America" made her a familiar name, and her unique and robust singing style brought joy to millions of folks at home despite their having good reason for despair.

That same infectious quality she brings to "Christmas Eve in My Home Town", an underestimated holiday song by Stan Zabka and Don Upton that was first published in 1951 during the height of the Korean War. The song, at first, was quite popular when it was dubbed by Armed Forces Radio as the "GI Christmas Song". Zabka, who worked for the Armed Forces Network as a military news chief during the war, later composed such songs and instrumental works as "Take Thou My Heart", "Searching Wind", "Razz Ma Tazz", and the "Chimes" theme for the original Tonight Show on NBC, a television network with which he was long associated.

Zabka and Upton paint a lovely backdrop of small town people congregating on quaint village squares while church bells are ringing. This is nostalgic imagery at its best, one which resonates with a simple beauty. Kate Smith helps to make the song more endearing. Through the magic of her voice, wonderful holiday scenes from our home towns, no matter where they are, come alive whether in reality or in our dreams.

> There's so much to remember!
> No wonder I remember
> Christmas Eve in My Home Town.
>
> Carols in the square,
> Laughter everywhere,
> Couples kissing under the mistletoe.
> I can't help reminiscing,
> Knowing I'll be missing
> Christmas Eve in My Home Town.
> Nothing can erase
> Mem'ries I embrace
> Those familiar footprints up on the snow!
> There's so much to remember!
> No wonder I remember
> Christmas Eve in My Home Town.

I like to be there,
Trimming the tree there,
And there's a chance that I might!
I can hear singing,
Steeple bells ringing
Noel and Silent Night.
Wise men journeyed far
Guided by a star,
But, though I'm not a wise man,
This I know:
Through dreams and just pretending,
I'm there and I'll be spending
Christmas Eve in My Home Town.

Christmas Eve in My
Hometown
detail of illustration from
LIFE, *December 21, 1950*
Kenneth W. Thompson
(b.1907)

Recording Artist—
Bing Crosby

Words—
John Redmond
(1906-1982),
James Cavanaugh
(1892-1967),
and Frank Weldon
(1903-1970),
American songwriters

Music—
James Cavanaugh
and Frank Weldon

With so many Americans of Irish descent, it was inevitable that some enterprising Irish-American songwriters would eventually compose a holiday song befitting their heritage. In 1950 "Christmas in Killarney", an upbeat song with a strong Irish jig flavor, was one of four new American Christmas songs that made their debuts that year. Most of them went on to become holiday standards.

Percy Faith (1908-1976), a Canadian-born conductor noted for his full mellow sounds, along with his orchestra and the Shillelagh Singers produced the original recording of "Christmas in Killarney" in 1950. A year later the song was introduced to American radio by Dennis Day (1917-1988), a highly respected Irish tenor who had a long association with Jack Benny's radio show.

John Redmond, James Cavanaugh, and Frank Weldon, our enterprising Irish-Americans, collaborated to create a holiday song that would interpret their own wistful views of Christmas on the "Old Sod". Bing Crosby, another Irish-American and one of the most popular singers in America at the time, gives "Christmas in Killarney" a ring of authenticity.

The result of all these efforts is a charming song that depicts the scenery of southwestern Ireland in a bouncy, rhythmic, and cheery way. Note how such holiday symbols as mistletoe and Santa Claus are given the Irish treatment.

"Christmas in Killarney"
1950 sheet music cover
National Museum of
American History,
Smithsonian Institution

The holly green, the ivy green,
The prettiest picture you've ever seen
Is Christmas in Killarney
With all of the folks at home.

It's nice, you know, to kiss your beau
While cuddling under the mistletoe,
And Santa Claus you know, of course,
Is one of the boys from home.

The door is always open;
The neighbors pay a call;
And Father John before he's gone
Will bless the house and all.

How grand it feels to click your heels
And join in the fun of the jigs and reels;
I'm handing you no blarney,
The likes you've never known
Is Christmas in Killarney
With all of the folks at home.

10 ✳ *The Christmas Song*

Other Title—
Chestnuts Roasting on an
Open Fire

Recording Artist—
Nat "King" Cole

Words—
Robert Wells (1922-1998),
American composer, author,
and producer

Music—
Mel Torme (1925-1999),
American composer, singer,
drummer, and actor

A truly delightful holiday song, "The Christmas Song" was the collaborative effort of Mel Torme and his longtime friend, Robert Wells, during the summer of 1946. They accomplished this despite a terrific heat spell that was besieging Los Angeles.

Torme, a Chicago-born jazz-style singer, and a World War II Air Force veteran, was called "Velvet Fog" at an early time in his career when he was singing more sentimental songs. He never liked that label, and he eventually progressed from a popular singer to one of the most unique and supreme jazz singers of his time, one with a lot of heart and great sense of timing. A composer, who also loved classical music, Torme wrote some 300 songs, more than half with Robert Wells. He was part of a pre-rock generation of songwriters that produced lyrics marked by grace, wit, charm, and intelligence. His passing was mourned by many who were nostalgic for an age when songwriters showed remarkable lyric writing skills and style.

Soon after completion of "The Christmas Song", Torme approached Nat "King" Cole (1919-1965), an African-American singer, jazz composer, and conductor, about recording "The Christmas Song". Cole, at the time noted for his jazz style of singing, felt the song should be performed with string instruments predomi-

Tiny Tots with Eyes All
Aglow
illustration from LIFE
November 27, 1950

nant, but his record company rejected the idea. A recording of the song with his own jazz group did not suit Cole's taste, and he eventually had the song rearranged for strings as he had first wanted. It was Cole's exquisite recording that popularized the song, and over the years "The Christmas Song" has consistently ranked as one of the top-selling Christmas songs.

Considered an historic recording, it was honored, as was Torme himself for life time achievement in 1999, by the National Academy of Recording Arts & Sciences, or the Grammy Awards organization, by being inducted into its Hall of Fame. A tender and nostalgic composition with depth, "The Christmas Song" is one of America's classic holiday songs.

Chestnuts roasting on an open fire,
Jack Frost nipping at your nose,
Yuletide carols being sung by a choir
And folks dressed up like Eskimos.
Ev'rybody knows a turkey and some mistletoe
Help to make the season bright.
Tiny tots with their eyes all aglow
Will find it hard to sleep tonight.
They know that Santa's on his way;
He's loaded lots of toys and goodies on his sleigh.
And ev'ry mother's child is gonna spy
To see if reindeer really know how to fly.
And so I'm offering this simple phrase
To kids from one to ninety-two;
Although it's been said many times, many ways,
"Merry Christmas to you."

11 The Christmas Waltz

Recording Artist—
Robert Goulet

Words—
Sammy Cahn (1913-1993),
American lyricist

Music—
Jule Styne (1905-1994),
American songwriter

"The Christmas Waltz", a carefree seasonal song, was first published in 1954, a time when the long-playing record (LP) had emerged as a major development in the music recording industry. It was one of a number of musical collaborations by Sammy Cahn and Jule Styne. Besides producing another Christmas holiday favorite titled "Let It Snow! Let It Snow! Let It Snow!", they composed such popular songs as "I'll Walk Alone", "I Fall in Love Too Easily", and "Three Coins in the Fountain", an Academy Award winner in 1954. Sammy Cahn was also responsible for writing three other "Best Song" Oscars—"Call Me Irresponsible", "High Hopes", and "Come Fly with Me", among the thirty that had received Academy Award nominations.

Frank Sinatra (1915-1998), perhaps the greatest American entertainer of the 20th century as well as a film star of note, affectionately known as "The Chairman of the Board", or "Ol' Blue Eyes", had sung a number of Cahn's songs during his eventful and storied career. Cahn, in fact, often wrote songs specifically with Sinatra in mind, as was the case in 1954 for "The Christmas Waltz", another delightful holiday song of merit that has been underestimated, despite Sinatra's popularity.

But the romantic impulses inherent in Cahn's simple lyrics are also captured by Robert Goulet (b. 1933), the American-born Canadian baritone, in his recording of it. Goulet, who became familiar to the American public after starring in *Camelot*, the enormously popular Broadway play often associated with the era of President John F. Kennedy (1917-1963), adds his own distinctive flavor, and because of it "The Christmas Waltz" will endure as part of the rich heritage of American Christmas recordings.

"It's That Time of Year",
cover of The Saturday
Evening Post
December 22, 1956
John Clymer (1907-1989)

Frosted window panes,
Candles gleaming inside,
Painted candy canes on the tree;
Santa's on his way,
He's filled his sleigh with things,
Things for you and for me.

It's that time of year,
When the world falls in love,
Ev'ry song you hear seems to say:
"Merry Christmas,
May your New Year dreams come true."

And this song of mine,
in three quarter time,
Wishes you and yours
the same thing too.

12 Cowboy Carol

Other Title—
*There'll Be a New World
Beginnin' from Tonight*

Recording Artists—
*Hallé Orchestra & Chorus;
Arrangement by
Sir Malcolm Sargent*

Words & Music—
*Cecil A. Broadhurst, (1908-
1981), Canadian-born
American composer, violin-
ist, playwright, and painter*

The concluding song of a 1944 one-act play called *The Cowboy Christmas*, this lively carol was first performed in the Grand Ballroom of the Bellevue Stratford Hotel in Philadelphia. In the audience were representatives of labor and management from a local shipyard. The yard, under contract to supply vital war material to the U. S. government, was shut down due to a bitter strike, the timing of which posed a severe problem since it came at a critical stage of World War II. But the performance of *The Cowboy Christmas* reportedly created an atmosphere that brought executives of both sides together, and soon after the strike was settled.

For a number of years *The Cowboy Christmas* was performed worldwide in theaters, schools, churches and more unique places. One such production was held in a soccer stadium in Brazil with a cast that included mounted horsemen and music supplied by a large chorus and orchestra.

The play's theme song "Cowboy Carol" would be included each December as part of a world broadcast by the Royal Choral Society of London, conducted by Sir Malcolm Sargent (1895-1967) and accompanied by the London Philharmonic Orchestra, after its first performance and recording of Cecil Broadhurst's song in 1949. The carol became quite popular in England, and elsewhere around the world, following this recording. But the oldest tune for "Cowboy Carol" was actually composed in 1942 by Frances Roots Hadden (1910-2000), an American pianist and music educator, as part of a musical collaboration she had with Broadhurst.

*Caroling Neighbors, c.1950
American Christmas card
Arthur J. FitzSimmons
(1909-1984)
Leanin' Tree Museum of
Western Art*

Broadhurst, a versatile artist who wrote more than 100 country and western songs, energizes "Cowboy Carol" with a rugged, though tender, lilt. The panoramic backdrop could have come from his native Canada and its prairies or from the southwestern United States where he resided. The theme of the play deals with three cowboys, camped with their cattle, as they follow a strange, luminous, and bright star that leads them to a barn where a manger scene is revealed. Once there they sense the beginning of something new and special for the world.

REFRAIN:
There'll be a new world beginnin' from t'night!
There'll be a new world beginnin' from t'night!
When I climb up on my saddle
Gonna take Him to my heart!
There'll be a new world beginnin' from t'night!

A Silent Night in the West
c.1949
American Christmas card
Robert Lorenz (1922-1965)
Leanin' Tree Museum of
Western Art

Right across the prairie,
Clear across the valley,
Straight across the heart of ev'ry man,
There'll be a right new brand of livin'
That'll sweep like lightnin' fire
And take away the hate in every land.
    REFRAIN:

Right across the prairie,
Clear across the valley,
Straight across the heart of ev'ry man,
There'll be a right new brand of livin'
That'll sweep like lightnin' fire
And take away the hate in every land.
    REFRAIN:

Yay! Yippee! We're gonna ride the trail.
Yay! Yippee! We're gonna ride today!
When I climb up on my saddle
Gonna take Him to my heart!
There'll be a new world beginnin' from tonight.

13 ✳ A Cradle in Bethlehem

Recording Artist—
Nat "King" Cole

Words & Music—
Larry Stock (1896-1984),
American songwriter
and concert pianist
Alfred Bryan (1871-1958),
Canadian-born
American songwriter

"A Cradle in Bethlehem" is a fine musical account of the Nativity scene, evoking the simple phrasing and temperament of earlier lullaby carols of the 15th and 16th centuries. Its creators, Larry Stock, who co-wrote the popular song "Blueberry Hill", and Alfred Bryan, a very productive songwriter perhaps best known for his co-authorship of the very popular "Peg of My Heart", collaborated to produce a musical gem that was first published in 1952.

Nat "King" Cole (1919-1965), probably America's most popular African-American singer at the time, first heard the carol while on a trip to England. Cole was supposedly quite taken by the carol's emotional and overall quality, and he was happy to record it just as he had recorded other Christmas songs of both a religious and a secular nature.

By gently lending his rich baritone voice to the lovely lyrics, the legendary singer brings subtlety to the black spiritual idiom that is captured in the first stanza and its subsequent refrain. Furthermore, his reference to Old Testament prophecy fulfills the promise of Christian redemption, thus bringing full circle the blessed story that unfolded in Bethlehem.

A Cradle in Bethlehem,
c.1950
Lauren Ford (1893-1973)
Private Collection

Sing sweet and low a lullaby
'til angels say "Amen."
A mother tonight is rocking
A cradle in Bethlehem.

While wise men follow through the dark,
A star beckons them.
A mother tonight is rocking
A cradle in Bethlehem.

A little child shall lead them,
The prophets said of old,
In storm and tempest heed them
Until the bell is tolled.

Sing sweet and low a lullaby
'til angels say "Amen."
A mother tonight is rocking
A cradle in Bethlehem.

14 *Do You Hear What I Hear?*

Recording Artist—
Andy Williams;
Arranged & conducted by
Robert Mersey

Words & Music—
Gloria Shayne (b.1923)
and Noel Regney (b.1922),
American songwriters

An inspired carol published in 1962, "Do You Hear What I Hear?" emulates the spontaneity of ancient shepherd songs in telling the story of the Nativity. Slowly the tale unfolds with the night wind whispering the news of the birth of Christ to a little lamb. The lamb bleats the same message to the shepherd, and the shepherd then to his King. The music, meanwhile, grows in volume until it reaches a joyful crescendo. Andy Williams (b.1930), an American singer popular in the 1960s and 1970s and still active today, helps to make the carol more endearing with his soft inflections.

"Do You Hear What I Hear?" has gained a measure of popularity in the United States since its first printing. Well crafted by Gloria Shayne and Noel Regney, its humble message is characterized by simple poetry and a clarity of purpose, quite reminiscent of the lyrical carol gems that have sparkled over the centuries like brilliant stars in the heavens.

The Shepherd Boy, c.1955
Lauren Ford (1893-1973)
Private Collection

Said the night wind to the little lamb,
"Do you see what I see?
Way up in the sky little lamb?"
"Do you see what I see?"
A star, a star, dancing in the night
With a tail as big as a kite,
With a tail as big as a kite.

Said the little lamb to the shepherd boy,
"Do you hear what I hear
Ringing through the skies shepherd boy?"
"Do you hear what I hear?"
A song, a song, high above the trees
With a voice as big as the sea,
With a voice as big as the sea.

Said the shepherd boy to the Mighty King,
"Do you know what I know
In Your palace-warm Mighty King?"
"Do you know what I know?"
A child, a child, shivers in the cold,
Let us bring Him silver and gold,
Let us bring Him silver and gold.

Said the King to the People everywhere,
"Listen to what I say;
Pray for peace, people everywhere!"
"Listen to what I say!"
The Child, the Child, sleeping in the night,
He will bring us goodness and light,
He will bring us goodness and light.

"Do you hear what I hear?"
"Do you hear what I hear?"

15 * Frosty the Snow Man

Recording Artists—
Gene Autry with The Cass County Boys; Orchestra conducted by Carl Cotner

Words—
Walter E. Rollins (1906-1973), American songwriter

Music—
Steve E. Nelson (b.1907), American songwriter and composer

Gene Autry (1907-1998), the famous American country-western singer and singing cowboy movie star, made a recording of this jolly 1950 song in 1951 when it rose to number seven on the pop music charts. Nat "King" Cole (1919-1965) also had a hit with his 1951 rendition. Autry, whose death came soon after that of Roy Rogers (1912-1998), another popular American singing cowboy and television favorite, would later become a successful businessman as the owner of several radio and TV shows and the California Angels baseball team.

Steve Nelson, the song's composer, was noted for his country, children, and holiday songs. "Frosty the Snow Man" would become his greatest single hit record and would inspire at least three television cartoon specials. Essentially a seasonal song for children, "Frosty the Snow Man" has a carefree, playful air, and possesses

Snow Sculpturing
from a 1952 calendar
Norman Rockwell (1894-1978)

elements of a fairy tale. Notice how Frosty begins to melt in the hot sun and must run away, with a promise to return some day.

> Frosty the Snow Man was a jolly, happy soul
> With a corncob pipe and a button nose
> And his eyes made out of coal.
> Frosty the Snow Man made the children laugh and play.
> Were they surprised when before their eyes
> How he came to life that day.
> There must have been some magic in
> That old silk hat they found,
> For when they placed it on his head,
> He began to dance around.
> Oh, Frosty the Snow Man was alive as he could be,
> And the children say he could laugh
> And play just the same as you and me.
>
> Frosty the Snow Man knew the sun was hot that day,
> So he said, "Let's run and we'll have fun
> Before I melt away."
> So down to the village with a broomstick in his hand,
> Running here and there all around the square,
> Sayin', "Catch me if you can."
> He led them down the streets of town
> Right to a traffic cop,
> And he only paused a moment
> When he heard him holler, "Stop!"
> For Frosty the Snow Man had to hurry on his way,
> But he waved good-bye, sayin',
> "Don't you cry; I'll be back again someday."
>
> There must have been some magic in
> That old silk hat they found,
> For when they placed it on his head,
> He began to dance around.
> Oh, Frosty the Snow Man was alive as he could be,
> And the children say he could laugh
> And play just the same as you and me.
>
> Thumpety thump thump, thumpety thump thump,
> Look at Frosty go;
> Thumpety thump thump, thumpety thump thump,
> Over the hills of snow.

16 ✳ *Go Tell It on the Mountain*

Recording Artists—

The Westminster Choir College: Joseph Flummerfelt, conductor; Daniel Beckwith, organist; Nancy Tenore, soprano; Jeffrey Martin, tenor

Words & Music —

Anonymous late 19th- or early 20th-century American spiritual folk, possibly by Frederick Jerome Work (1880-1942), African-American composer, teacher, and scholar

Two members of the Work family have connections to this remarkable song. Both Frederick Jerome Work and his nephew, John W. Work, Jr. (1871-1925), were scholars who collected and promoted Negro spirituals. Frederick may have been the creator of this exceptional song, and John, perhaps inspired by an old spiritual titled "When I Was a Seeker", arranged the melody and adapted the words for the first publication of "Go Tell It on the Mountain".

John Wesley Work, Jr. found sustenance for his music endeavors from his student days at Fisk University, an eminent institution established in 1866 for the education of freed slaves and one noted for the introduction of the Fisk University Jubilee Singers onto the world stage. This renowned group was formed in 1871 to raise scholarship money for the school after it was almost forced to shut down due to lack of financial support. The Jubilee Singers (who took their name from the year of freedom in the Bible) were quite successful on their tours of the United States and Europe, and in the process they raised the Negro spiritual to an art form. While on tour, particularly in their own country, they were sometimes treated unfairly, suffering the indignity of being turned away or thrown out

The Lord Is My Shepherd
1863 oil on wood
Eastman Johnson (1824-1906)
National Museum of American Art, Smithsonian Institution

of hotels, ship cabins, railway stations, and even churches, because of the color of their skin. But stout-hearted and undaunted, the singing group persisted, thus immortalizing America's great spiritual heritage.

Many of the spirituals the Works collected had originally been sung by their forebears as they toiled in the fields, or at difficult manual labor, during the dark time of slavery. It was one way of establishing relationships and feeling that God was near. The story of Christmas, of God's Son being born as man to redeem and free man of his sins, was important in itself and as a symbol of hope in their quest for freedom. In this recording of "Go Tell It on the Mountain" one might detect notes of hope and courage, as well as a sense of joy with which people celebrate the promise of a new beginning, just as poor shepherds from the fields of Bethlehem once did beside the manger.

"Where the Shepherds All Seen the Star"
1942, ink on paper
Allan Rohan Crite (b.1916),
African-American
The Montclair Art Museum

REFRAIN:
Go tell it on the mountain,
Over the hills and everywhere,
Go tell it on the mountain
That Jesus Christ is born.

While shepherds kept their watching
O'er silent flocks by night,
Behold throughout the heavens
There shone a holy light.
    REFRAIN:

The shepherds feared and trembled
When lo! above the earth
Rang out the angel chorus
That hailed our Savior's birth.
    REFRAIN:

And lo, when they had heard it,
They all bowed down and prayed;
They traveled on together
To where the Babe was laid.
REFRAIN:

Down in a lowly manger
The humble Christ was born,
And God sent us salvation
That blessed Christmas morn.
REFRAIN:

Recording Artist—
Andy Williams;
Arranged & conducted by
Robert Mersey

Words—
Ralph Blane (1914-1995),
American songwriter

Music—
Hugh Martin (b.1914),
American composer,
arranger, and singer

"Have Yourself a Merry Little Christmas" is a wistful Christmas song written during World War II as a part of the musical score for the film *Meet Me in St. Louis.* This 1944 movie starred the irrepressible actress Judy Garland (1922-1969), who was noted for her crowd-pleasing entertainment and singing and whose role in another film, *The Wizard of Oz,* has been annually reprised in the United States since the early days of television.

The song's composers, Ralph Blane and Hugh Martin, went on to become song-writing partners for a number of musical television shows and choral works over the years. As a result of their collaborative spirit, "Have Yourself a Merry Little Christmas" has the sweet embrace of nostalgia. This effect was more pronounced because of the tribulations of World War II, especially for Americans whose sons and daughters were fighting the good fight against fascist forces in Europe and Asia. Even today the song's special quality still holds true.

Have yourself a merry little Christmas;
Let your heart be light.
From now on, our troubles will be out of sight.
Have yourself a merry little Christmas;
Make the Yuletide gay.
From now on, our troubles will be miles away.

Here we are as in olden days, happy golden days of yore;
Faithful friends who are dear to us gather
    near to us once more.
Through the years we all will be together
If the Fates allow.
Hang a shining star upon the highest bough,
And have yourself a merry little Christmas now.

Union Station
cover of The Saturday Evening Post
December 23, 1944
Norman Rockwell (1894-1978)

Here Comes Santa Claus

Recording Artists—
Gene Autry with vocal
group

Words & Music —
Gene Autry (1907-1998),
American country-western
singer, cowboy movie star,
and songwriter;
Oakley Haldeman (1909-
1986), American composer
and publisher

"Here Comes Santa Claus" is a light-hearted children's Christmas song that reflects the gaiety in the United States in the immediate years after World War II. Written in 1946, its focus is the cheery arrival of Santa Claus and his reindeer. Gene Autry made the song a popular hit the following year. For several years the song did well on the pop music charts, reaching its highest level in 1949. Since Autry's recording, a number of other popular artists have released their own versions of his catchy tune.

The theme of Santa bearing gifts is rooted in one of several legends about St. Nicholas the Bishop of Myra (d. 350 A.D). St. Nicholas reputedly inherited his family wealth and was known to have been quite generous toward children. Such acts eventually earned him the title of Patron Saint of Children.

Here comes Santa Claus, here comes Santa Claus
Right down Santa Claus Lane.
Vixen and Blitzen and all his reindeer
        are pulling on the rein.
Bells are ringing, children singing;
All is merry and bright.
Hang your stockings and say your pray'rs,
'Cause Santa Claus comes tonight.

Here comes Santa Claus, here comes Santa Claus
Right down Santa Claus Lane.
He's got a bag that is filled with toys
        for the girls and boys again.

"Here Comes Santa Claus"
1947 sheet music cover
National Museum of American
History, Smithsonian Institution

Santa, c.1945
gouache & oil
on illustration board
Tran J. Mawicke (b.1911)

Hear those sleigh bells jingle jangle,
What a beautiful sight.
Jump in bed, cover up your head,
'Cause Santa Claus comes tonight.

Here comes Santa Claus, here comes Santa Claus
Right down Santa Claus Lane.
He doesn't care if you're rich or poor
    for he loves you just the same.
Santa knows that we're God's children;
That makes ev'rything right.
Fill your hearts with a Christmas cheer,
'Cause Santa Claus comes tonight.

Here comes Santa Claus, here comes Santa Claus
Right down Santa Claus Lane.
He'll come around when the chimes ring out;
    then it's Christmas morn again.
Peace on earth will come to all
If we just follow the light.
Let's give thanks to the Lord above,
'Cause Santa Claus comes tonight.

Recording Artist—
*Kate Smith;
Arranged & conducted by
Peter Matz*

Words—
*Henry Wadsworth
Longfellow (1807-1882),
American poet; adapted by
Johnny Marks*

Music—
*Johnny Marks (1909-1985),
American songwriter and
music publisher*

"I Heard the Bells on Christmas Day" is a hopeful song that initially sprang from a well of despair. The carol words come from the poem "Christmas Bells" by Henry Wadsworth Longfellow that was composed on Christmas day in 1863, a time when Longfellow was grieving upon learning that his son, a lieutenant in the Army of the Potomac during the Civil War, had been wounded in battle. The famous poet, still in a state of depression over his wife's death from several years earlier, set out wanting to write a poem about his feelings. But upon hearing Christmas bells, Longfellow's demeanor changed, and thus what had begun with a sense of melancholy ended on a more hopeful note.

John Baptiste Calkin (1827-1905), an English organist, composed the original bell-like music for "I Heard the Bells on Christmas Day" around 1872, although it may have been someone else who combined the words and music. A more recent tune was composed by Johnny Marks in 1956 and recorded by his good friend, Bing Crosby (1904-1977).

On a lighter note, when the record company was preparing to release Crosby's recording, one of its secretaries called Marks' publishing company to get infor-

The Field Hospital
*1867 oil on paperboard
mounted on plywood
Eastman Johnson (1824-1906)
Museum of Fine Art, Boston*

mation for the record label. "Of course we know who Johnny is," the secretary said, "but who is this Longfellow lyricist?"

> I heard the bells on Christmas Day
> Their old familiar carols play,
> And wild and sweet the words repeat
> Of peace on earth, goodwill to men.
>
> I thought as now this day had come,
> The belfries of all Christendom
> Had rung so long the unbroken song
> Of peace on earth, goodwill to men.
>
> And in despair I bowed my head;
> "There is no peace on earth," I said,
> "For hate is strong and mocks the song
> Of peace on earth, goodwill to men."
>
> Then pealed the bells more loud and deep:
> "God is not dead, nor doth He sleep;
> The wrong shall fail, the right prevail
> With peace on earth goodwill to men."

Facing page:
Civil War Christmas Eve
from Harper's Weekly,
*December 1862
Thomas Nast (1840-1902)*

"Peace on the Earth, Good Will to Men."

"Peace on the Earth,
Good Will to Men"
*illustration from 1942 carol
songbook*

Based on the poem "Christmas Bells":

I heard the bells on Christmas Day
Their old, familiar carols play,
       And wild and sweet
       The words repeat
Of peace on earth, good-will to men!

And thought how, as the day had come,
The belfries of all Christendom
       Had rolled along
       Th' unbroken song
Of peace on earth, good-will to men!

Till, ringing, singing on its way,
The world revolved from night to day,
       A voice, a chime,
       a chant sublime,
Of peace on earth, good-will to men!

Then from each black, accursed mouth
The cannon thundered in the South,
       And with the sound
       The carols drowned
Of peace on earth, good-will to men!

It was as if an earthquake rent
The hearthtones of a continent,
       And made forlorn
       The household born
Of peace on earth, good-will to men!

And in despair I bowed my head:
"There is no peace on earth," I said,
       "For hate is strong,
       And mocks the song
Of peace on earth, good-will to men!"

Then pealed the bells more loud and deep:
"God is not dead, nor doth He sleep!
       The Wrong shall fail,
       The Right prevail,
With peace on earth, good-will to men!"

20 I Wonder As I Wander

Recording Artist—
Mahalia Jackson;
Orchestra under the direc-
tion of Sid Bass

Words & Music—
John Jacob Niles
(1892-1980), American
folksinger, composer, and
collector of folk songs

Published in the 1934 volume *Songs of the Hill-Folk*, the Appalachian folk song "I Wonder As I Wander" was collected by John Jacob Niles, a pre-eminent American folklorist. Niles first heard the carol a year earlier while attending a meeting of evangelists in Murphy, a small North Carolina town. During that session a young girl stood up and sang "I Wonder As I Wander" without any musical accompaniment. On the spur of the moment, and on subsequent occasions, Niles asked the girl to sing the carol until he had accurately written down the lyrics and tune.

One of the finest American folk carols discovered in the 20th century, although it may have originated from an anonymous 19th-century composer, "I Wonder As I Wander" is the end product of Niles' unique ability to quickly improvise, something he was able to perfect because of his own musical shorthand system.

Due to his persistence, a most haunting and beautiful carol was fashioned, especially as it is performed by the great gospel singer Mahalia Jackson (1911-1972). Her magnificent voice energizes Niles' folk classic and adds resonance to its simple poetry by harking to one special day, many centuries ago, when poor ordinary people beheld a newborn child in the most humble surroundings.

Ruby Green Singing
1928 oil on canvas
James Chapin (1887-1975)
Norton Museum of Art

I wonder as I wander out under the sky
How Jesus the Savior did come for to die
For poor on'ry people like you and like I;
I wonder as I wander out under the sky.

When Mary birthed Jesus, 'twas in a cow's stall,
With wise men and farmers and shepherds and all.
But high from God's heaven, a star's light did fall,
And the promise of ages it then did recall.

When Jesus had wanted for any wee thing,
A star in the sky or a bird on the wing,
Or all of God's angels in heav'n for to sing,
He surely could have it, 'cause He was the King.

I wonder as I wander out under the sky
How Jesus the Savior did come for to die
For poor on'ry people like you and like I;
I wonder as I wander out under the sky.

Recording Artist—
Chet Akins

Words—
Kim Gannon (1900-1974),
American poet

Music—
Walter Kent (1911-1994),
American musician and
composer

James Kimball (Kim) Gannon composed his best-known poem "I'll Be Home for Christmas" in 1943. In the same year Walter Kent collaborated with him to write the music. Their friendly effort produced one of the most nostalgic of all World War II period songs. Bing Crosby (1904-1977), one of the top recording artists in the country, helped to make it an instant big seller.

It is not too difficult to imagine how American fighting boys must have felt at Christmas during one of the 20th century's most difficult periods. How they must have pined to be home for the holidays, instead of off in foreign territories either hunkered down on some desolate battlefield or sailing the turbulent waters of the world's oceans.

The brief "I'll Be Home for Christmas" certainly packs an emotional wallop with its wistful, almost bittersweet, and haunting lyrics. Even today it would not be a far stretch to suggest that whenever people are away during the holidays, this special Christmas song might be on the lips of those who gaze homeward.

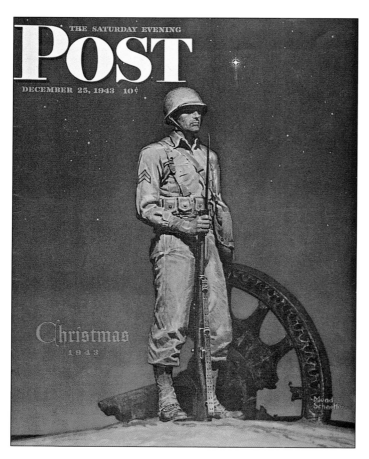

Christmas 1943 *cover of*
The Saturday Evening Post
December 25, 1943
Mead Schaeffer (1898-1980)

I'll be home for Christmas;
You can count on me.
Please have snow and mistletoe
And presents on the tree.
Christmas Eve will find me
Where the love-light gleams.
I'll be home for Christmas
If only in my dreams.

Other Title—
It Came Upon a Midnight Clear

Recording Artists—
Mormon Tabernacle Choir;
Richard P. Condie, director

Words—
Edmund Hamilton Sears
(1810-1876),
American clergyman

Music—
Richard Storrs Willis
(1919-1900), American
composer and music critic

Written as a poem by Edmund H. Sears on a cold December day in 1849, "It Came Upon the Midnight Clear" was published that same month in the *Christian Register*, a church magazine. A year later, Richard Storrs Willis wrote a flowing melody under the title "Study No. 23" in his *Church Chorals* and also *Choir Studies*, a piece of music that would soon be attached to Sears' lyrics. Willis, an editor and music critic for the *New York Tribune* at the time, had a different hymn in mind when he first composed the music. Later, after he had finished his studies at Yale University, he went on to study music in Europe under the German composer Felix Mendelssohn.

The Rev. Sears, a farmer's son and direct descendant of one of the original Pilgrim Fathers, was pastor of the Unitarian Church in Wayland, Massachusetts. He loved poems, having begun writing verse at the age of ten and reciting it during his moments of solitude. His poetic carol is particularly noteworthy for its incorporation of the theme of peace among men and nations—a sentiment hardly mentioned in other carols of the day. Also, the carol does not make any direct reference to the birth of Christ. Originally the carol was five stanzas long; the fourth stanza is generally omitted in most hymnals.

Glad Tidings, *c.1880-1885*
American Christmas card
National Museum of American
History, Smithsonian Institution

It came upon the midnight clear,
That glorious song of old,
From angels bending near the earth,
To touch their harps of gold:
"Peace on the earth, good will to men,
From heaven's all-gracious King."
The world in solemn stillness lay,
To hear the angels sing.

Still through the cloven skies they come
With peaceful wings unfurled,
And still their heavenly music floats
O'er all the weary world;
Above its sad and lowly plains
They bend on hovering wing,
And ever o'er its Babel sounds
The blessed angels sing.

Yet with the woes of sin and strife
The world hath suffered long;
Beneath the angel-strain have rolled
Two thousand years of wrong;

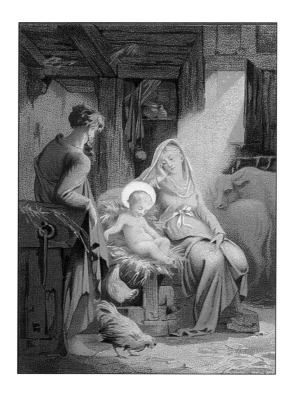

Emmanuel
c.1880-1885 antique American
Christmas card
National Museum of American
History, Smithsonian Institution

And man, at war with man, hears not
The love song which they bring;
O hush the noise, ye men of strife,
And hear the angels sing.

O ye, beneath life's crushing load,
Whose forms are bending low,
Who toil along the climbing way
With painful steps and slow,
Look now! for glad and golden hours
Come swiftly on the wing;
O rest beside the weary road
And hear the angels sing!

For lo! the days are hastening on,
By prophet-bards foretold,
When with the ever-circling years
Comes round the age of gold;
When peace shall over all the earth
Its ancient splendors fling,
And the whole world give back the song
Which now the angels sing.

Recording Artist—
Kate Smith;
Arranged & conducted by
Peter Matz

Words & Music—
Meredith Willson (1902-
1984), American lyricist,
flutist, and conductor

Meredith Willson, an excellent songwriter best known for his 1957 Broadway musical *The Music Man*, published "It's Beginning to Look Like Christmas" in 1951. The song has a strong nostalgic appeal, one quite typical of the superior post-World War II American holiday compositions. Like other new popular songs, it was sung by a number of American recording artists, including the ever-popular Kate Smith (1909-1986).

An authentic American institution, who helped to raise more money for U.S. bonds during World War II than any other recording artist, Kate Smith had a robust singing style that made her a favorite of the immense radio listening audience of the 1940s and early 1950s. Who could ever forget her rousing rendition of "God Bless America"? Her infectious spirit is quite pervasive, embellishing "It's Beginning to Look Like Christmas" with a down-home flavor that most Americans can readily appreciate.

It's beginning to look like Christmas
Ev'rywhere you go;
Take a look in the five-and-ten,
Glistening once again
With candy canes and silver lanes aglow.

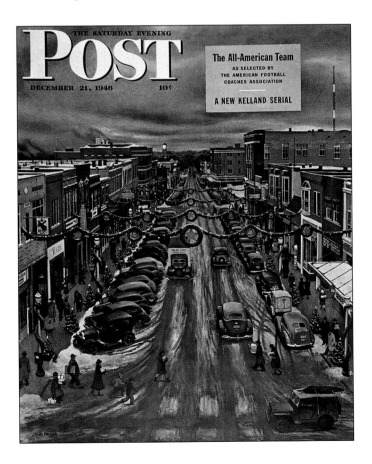

Falls City, Nebraska
cover of The Saturday
Evening Post
December 21, 1946
John Falter (1910-1982)

It's beginning to look like Christmas,
Toys in ev'ry store,
But the prettiest sight to see
Is the holly that will be
On your own front door.

A pair of hopalong boots
And a pistol that shoots
Is the wish of Barney and Ben;
Dolls that will talk
And will go for a walk
Is the hope of Janice and Jen;
And Mom and Dad can hardly wait
For school to start again.

It's beginning to look a lot like Christmas
Ev'rywhere you go;
There's a tree in the Grand Hotel,
One in the park as well.
The sturdy kind that doesn't mind the snow.
It's beginning to look like Christmas;
Soon the bells will start,
And the thing that will make them ring
Is the carol that you sing
Right within your heart.

Recording Artist—
The Mariners

Words & Music—
John Jacob Niles
(1892-1980), American
folk singer, composer, and
folk song collector

"Jesus, Jesus, Rest Your Head" is a charming folk carol that comes from the southern Appalachian Mountains region, most likely Kentucky. Written in 1932, it was published three years later by John Jacob Niles, a master collector of American folk tunes and a strong proponent of Americans discovering their own folk music roots. Niles was often inspired by the songs he heard in Appalachia. It was common for him upon hearing a new tune to jot it down on paper immediately, a practice similar to that of Ralph Vaughan Williams (1872-1958), an eminent English composer and another avid collector of folk songs.

A fine example of rural American folk carols, "Jesus, Jesus, Rest Your Head" is simple, direct, genuine, and humble—essential qualities of carol gems from the English countryside of the 14th and 15th century. What makes the carol even more endearing is the air of serenity it creates about a stirring event that took place in a poor stable a very long time ago. In an unobtrusive and gentle way, it also reminds us of the true relevance of Christmas.

With Babe on Her Knee,
1912 book illustration
Florence Edith Storer
(active 1900-1915)

Jesus, Jesus, rest Your head,
You have got a manger bed.
All the evil folk on earth
Sleep on feathers at their birth.
Jesus, Jesus, rest Your head,
You have got a manger bed.

Have you heard about our Jesus?
Have you heard about his fate?
How his mother went to that stable
On that Christmas Eve so late?
Winds were blowing, cows were lowing,
Stars were glowing, glowing, glowing.
Jesus, Jesus, rest your head,
You have got a manger bed.

To that manger came the Wise Men,
Bringing things from here and yon
For the mother and the father
And the blessed little one.
Winds were blowing, cows were lowing,
Stars were glowing, glowing, glowing.
Jesus, Jesus, rest Your head,
You have got a manger bed.

Jesus, Jesus, rest Your head,
You have got a manger bed.
All the evil folk on earth
Sleep on feathers at their birth.
Jesus, Jesus, rest Your head,
You have got a manger bed.

25 ❄ *Jingle-Bell Rock*

Recording Artist—
Bobby Helms

Words & Music—
Joseph Carleton Beal
(1900-1967), American
songwriter, publisher,
and author;
James R. Boothe
(1917-1976), American
songwriter, journalist, and
advertising copywriter

"Jingle-Bell Rock" represents one of the first attempts to incorporate popular rock-and-roll music as part of the American Christmas song repertoire. Written in 1957, exactly 100 years after the composition of "Jingle Bells", which may not be totally coincidental, it immediately became a top-selling record when Bobby Helms' recording was released. Helms (b.1933), an American country singer, had been riding the crest of popularity that year, especially after his other pop hit titled "My Special Angel" sold over a million records.

The brainchild of the enterprising Joseph Carleton Beal and James R. Boothe, "Jingle-Bell Rock" alludes to the same holiday theme as its hundred-year-old predecessor, and it does so with a gentle, though more upbeat, modern flavor.

Jingle-bell, jingle-bell, jingle-bell rock,
Jingle bells swing and jingle bells ring.
Snowin' and blowin' up bushels of fun,
Now the jingle hop has begun.
Jingle-bell, jingle-bell, jingle-bell rock,
Jingle bells chime in jingle-bell time.
Dancin' and prancin' in Jingle Bell Square
In the frosty air.
What a bright time; it's the right time
To rock the night away.
Jingle-bell time is a swell time
To go glidin' in a one-horse sleigh.
Giddy-yap jingle horse; pick up your feet;
Jingle around the clock.
Mix and mingle in a jinglin' beat;
That's the jingle-bell rock.

Joy Ride, 1953
oil on pressed wood
Grandma Moses (1860-1961)
Grandma Moses Properties

26 ✳ *Jingle Bells*

Other Title—
One-Horse Open Sleigh

Recording Artist—
Burl Ives

Words & Music—
James S. Pierpont
(1822-1893), American
author and expert on
reading and recitation

Probably the best-known American secular Christmas song, "Jingle Bells" was written in 1857, or somewhat before by James S. Pierpont. It was first performed at a Thanksgiving program at his Boston church, where he also taught Sunday school. Pierpont was the son of John Pierpont (1785-1866), an abolitionist poet and minister, and the uncle of John Pierpont Morgan (1837-1913), the great American financier. (On an ironic note, James wrote several war songs during the Civil War that became popular with the Confederacy.) Initially titled "One-Horse Open Sleigh" the song was quickly learned by Pierpont's Sunday school children because his lyrics were so clear and simple.

There is an unsubstantiated anecdote claiming the title was changed to "Jingle Bells" because one of the composer's friends commented that the piece was a delightful jingle, but the many repetitions of the phrase made such a change entirely natural or even predictable. Judged by the number of recording artists who have released this catchy tune, "Jingle Bells" holds a very special place in the American holiday song repertoire and in the hearts of Christmas lovers.

REFRAIN:
Jingle bells, jingle bells,
jingle all the way;
Oh, what fun it is to ride
in a one-horse open sleigh.
Hey! jingle bells, jingle bells,
jingle all the way;
Oh! what fun it is to ride
in a one-horse open sleigh!

Dashing through the snow
In a one-horse open sleigh;
O'er the fields we go,
Laughing all the way.
Bells on bobtail ring,
Making spirits bright;
What fun it is to ride and sing
A sleighing song tonight.
    REFRAIN:

A day or two ago
I thought I'd take a ride,
And soon Miss Fannie Bright
Was seated by my side;
The horse was lean and lank,
Misfortune seem'd his lot,
He got into a drifted bank,
And then we got upsot!
REFRAIN:

Facing page:
A Christmas Party, *1853*
George Henry Durrie
(1820-1863)
The Thomas Gilcrease Institute
of American History and Art

Recording Artists—
Woody Herman & his Orchestra

Words—
Sammy Cahn (1913-1993), American lyricist

Music—
Jule Styne (1905-1994), American songwriter

Possessing a good deal of zest, "Let It Snow! Let It Snow! Let It Snow!" is another delightful holiday contribution from Sammy Cahn and Jule Styne. The two collaborated on a number of hit songs, including "I'll Walk Alone", "Three Coins in the Fountain", and "I Fall in Love Too Easily". Styne, whose career as a piano prodigy was cut short by a finger injury, wrote music that people could snap their fingers to. He composed a number of unforgettable songs such as "Diamonds Are a Girl's Best Friend", "The Party's Over", and "People" during his long Broadway career, which included long-running classics as *Gentlemen Prefer Blondes*, *Gypsy*, and *Funny Girl*.

First published in 1945, Cahn and Styne's song immediately caught the attention of several popular singers and soon rose to the number-one position on national music charts with the rich baritone rendition of Vaughn Monroe (1911-1973), a top American singer and band leader. Woody Herman (1913-1987), a "Big Band" jazz legend, later followed in 1946 with his recording of "Let It Snow! Let It Snow! Let It Snow!" Other recording artists who released the song in the same year were Connie Boswell (1907-1962) and Bob Crosby (b.1913).

Let It Snow!
illustration from
The Saturday Evening Post,
December 11, 1943

The backdrop of two people in love and the falling snow adds to the romance of "Let It Snow! Let It Snow! Let It Snow!", one of the most successful seasonal songs of the immediate post-World War II era.

Oh, the weather outside is frightful,
But the fire is so delightful,
And since we've no place to go,
Let it snow, let it snow, let it snow.

It doesn't show signs of stopping;
And I brought some corn for popping;
The lights are turned way down low,
Let it snow, let it snow, let it snow.

When we finally kiss good night,
How I'll hate going out in the storm;
But if you'll really hold me tight,
All the way home I'll be warm.

The fire is slowly dying,
And, my dear, we're still good-byeing,
But as long as you love me so,
Let it snow, let it snow, let it snow.

Back Home for Keeps
illustration from LIFE
October 18, 1943
Jon Whitcomb (1906-1988)

28 ❋ The Little Drummer Boy

Other Title—
Carol of the Drum

Recording Artist—
The Harry Simeone Chorale

Words—
*Katherine K. Davis
(1892-1980), American
author, songwriter, and
teacher*

Music—
*Katherine K. Davis; revised
in 1958 in collaboration
with Harry Simeone
(b.1911), American
composer and conductor,
and Henry Onorati
(b.1912), American
author and newspaper
reporter*

The touching setting about a poor boy who can offer the infant Jesus only his drum-playing as a gift makes for a truly humble and reverential carol, and in this spirit "The Little Drummer Boy" was published in 1941 under the title of "Carol of the Drum". It was written by Katherine K. Davis, a multifaceted woman who seventeen years later would join with Harry Simeone and Henry Onorati to slightly rework and arrange the music into the form we know today. The three collaborators also decided to substitute the original carol with a catchier title.

The concept of "The Little Drummer Boy" may have been modeled after the French drumming carol "Patapan" although the music itself may have been derived from a Spanish song titled "Tabolilleros". Released as a recording by the Harry Simeone Chorale in 1958, the same year as its revision, "The Little Drummer Boy" immediately became popular and eventually spawned two television specials, in 1967 and 1976, both using the song's name. Davis's tender rendering of this tale of a poor boy and Christ Child represents one of America's finer and more recent contributions to the international Christmas carol repertoire.

Come, they told me,
(Pa-rum-pum-pum-pum)
A newborn King to see;
(Pa-rum-pum-pum-pum)
Our finest gifts we bring
(Pa-rum-pum-pum-pum)
To lay before the King,
(Pa-rum-pum-pum-pum,

rum-pum-pum-pum,
rum-pum-pum-pum)
So to honor Him
(Pa-rum-pum-pum-pum)
When we come.

Little Baby (Baby Gesu)
(Pa-rum-pum-pum-pum)
I am a poor boy too;
(Pa-rum-pum-pum-pum)
I have no gift to bring
(Pa-rum-pum-pum-pum)
That's fit to give our King.
(Pa-rum-pum-pum-pum,
rum-pum-pum-pum,
rum-pum-pum-pum)
Shall I play for You
(Pa-rum-pum-pum-pum)
On my drum?

Mary nodded;
(Pa-rum-pum-pum-pum)
The ox and lamb kept time;
(Pa-rum-pum-pum-pum)
I played my drum for Him;
(Pa-rum-pum-pum-pum)
I played my best for him.
(Pa-rum-pum-pum-pum,
rum-pum-pum-pum,
rum-pum-pum-pum)
Then He smiled at me,
(Pa-rum-pum-pum-pum)
Me and my drum.

Facing page:
The Little Drummer Boy
1968 book illustration
Ezra Jack Keats (1916-1983)

29 *Mary Had a Baby*

Recording Artist—
The Riverside Choir

Words & Music —
Anonymous 18th-19th
century African-American
spiritual

Sunday Morning
print
Thomas Hart Benton
(1889-1975)

A personal song of black slaves, "Mary had a Baby" most likely originated from the island of St. Helena off the coast of South Carolina, although some authorities have confused it with another St. Helena, the tiny island between Africa and South America where Napoleon Bonaparte (1769-1821) was exiled until his death. The South Carolina coastal island may have also been the port of call where slavery was first introduced in America in 1526, long before the historically recognized date of 1619 at the Jamestown colony.

A carol with two lyrical texts celebrating the birth of Christ, "Mary Had a Baby" may date from the 18th century. Later it was probably sung at religious revival camp meetings where a "call and response" technique was utilized to unify the congregation in worship. After the Civil War, this musical style became more prevalent in black churches, especially those of the rural South, whose members had learned it from their ancestors, almost all of whom were slaves.

Black slaves learned songs orally: some from attendance at church services of their white owners, and as a way of learning to speak English. These church services were generally fundamentalist in nature, and the congregation often sang the hymns of the English composer Isaac Watts. An 1820 edition of Watts' hymns circulated widely throughout the South, gaining popularity among black slaves

who used its hymn texts as the basis for their spirituals. But their interpretations of these hymns were more closely aligned to the traditional African work song form of leader-and-chorus antiphonal singing, in which a line was sung by a group leader, or precentor, and then repeated by the congregation. When a new wave of religious fervor swept the South in 1845, open-air preaching by whites became more commonplace and it was soon imitated by black teachers, thus forming a vocal style of worship that can still be felt today.

The beauty of "Mary Had a Baby" is especially evident in the arrangement by William Dawson (1898-1990), an African-American composer, conductor, and trombonist from Alabama. Dawson, whose body of work included *Negro Folk Symphony* that premiered in 1934 by the Philadelphia Orchestra under the direction of the great Leopold Stokowski (1882-1977), often wrote in a Neo-Romantic style that employed black folk song idioms. Inspired by the majesty of the carol text, he adroitly used this musical technique to create a heightened sense of dignity and to glorify a mother and her newborn child despite the humble surroundings.

Mary had a baby, My Lord!
Oh, Mary had a Baby,
Mary had a Baby, My Lord!
Where was He born?
Born in a manger.
Oh, Mary had a Baby
Born in a manger, My Lord!

What did they call Him?
"King Jesus",
What did they call Him,
"King Jesus".
Oh, Mary had a Baby.
He was called "King Jesus".
Mary had a Baby, oh, yes!

He is called "King Jesus",
"Mighty Counsellor",
"King Emanuel", "Mighty God",
"Everlasting Father",
"Prince of Peace".
Mary had a Baby.
My Lord! My Lord!

O, Mary where is your Baby

"O' Mary Where Is Your Baby"
1942 ink on paper
Allan Rohan Crite (b.1916),
African-American
The Montclair Art Museum

Facing page:
Church of the Nativity, *1840*
David Roberts (1796-1864),
Scottish
Paisley Museum & Art Gallery

Variant Lyrics:

Mary had a baby, oh, Lord,
Mary had a baby, oh my Lord,
Mary had a baby, oh Lord,
People keep a-comin' an' the train done gone.

What did she name him? oh, Lord,
What did she name him? oh my Lord,
What did she name him? oh Lord,
People keep a-comin' an' the train done gone.

She named him Jesus, oh, Lord,
She named him Jesus, oh my Lord,
She named him Jesus, oh Lord,
People keep a-comin' an' the train done gone.

Now where was he born? oh, Lord,
Where was he born? oh my Lord,
Where was he born? oh Lord,
People keep a-comin' an' the train done gone.

Born in a stable, oh, Lord,
Born in a stable, oh my Lord,
Born in a stable, oh Lord,
People keep a-comin' an' the train done gone.

And where did she lay him? oh, Lord,
Where did she lay him? oh my Lord,
Where did she lay him? oh Lord,
People keep a-comin' an' the train done gone.

She laid him in a manger, oh, Lord,
Laid him in a manger, oh my Lord,
Laid him in a manger, oh Lord,
People keep a-comin' an' the train done gone.

Mary had a baby, oh, Lord,
Mary had a baby, oh my Lord,
Mary had a baby, oh Lord,
People keep a-comin' an' the train done gone.

30 O Little Town of Bethlehem

Recording Artist—
Ray Price

Words—
Phillips Brooks (1835-1893), American minister

Music—
Lewis Henry Redner (1831-1908), American church organist and real-estate executive

One of America's most beloved carols, "O Little Town of Bethlehem" was written as a poem by Phillips Brooks in 1868, when he was a young rector in Philadelphia, just three years after he had traveled to the Holy Land. There he was impressed by Christmas observances at the Church of the Nativity in Bethlehem. The children of his Sunday school were delighted with his poem, prompting the Rev. Brooks to persuade Lewis Redner, the church organist, to set it to music.

Redner put off composing the music until the very last moment; then, during the night, he had a dream that inspired him to begin work on his composition. Immediately upon arising, he wrote down the melody and offered it to the children the following morning. "O Little Town of Bethlehem" has since attained a lofty status in the international repertoire of traditional Christmas carols, and the unforgettable lyrics bring enchantment to the sacred story about a glorious starry night of long ago.

O little town of Bethlehem,
How still we see Thee lie!

Above the deep and dreamless sleep,
The silent stars go by;
Yet in thy dark streets shineth
The everlasting Light;
The hopes and fears of all the years
Are met in Thee tonight.

For Christ is born of Mary,
And gathered all above,
While mortals sleep, the angels keep,
Their watch of wondering love.
O morning stars, together
Proclaim the holy birth!
And praises sing to God the King,
And peace to men on earth.

How silently, how silently,
The wondrous gift is giv'n!
So God imparts to human hearts
The blessings of His heav'n.
No ear may hear His coming,
But in this world of sin,
Where meek souls will receive Him, still
The dear Christ enters in.

Where children pure and happy
Pray to the blessed Child,
Where misery cries out to Thee,
Son of the mother mild;
Where charity stands watching
And faith holds wide the door,
The dark night wakes, the glory breaks,
And Christmas comes once more.

O holy Child of Bethlehem!
Descend to us, we pray;
Cast out our sin and enter in,
Be born in us today.
We hear the Christmas angels
The great glad tidings tell;
O come to us, abide with us,
Our Lord Immanuel.

Recording Artist—
Brenda Lee

Words & Music—
Johnny Marks (1909-1985),
American songwriter
and music publisher

During the summer of 1958 Johnny Marks watched some teenagers dance to rock music as he was looking at fir trees surrounding the beach on which he was sunbathing. Rock-and-roll music, still in its infancy, was the rage at that time. The association of the fir trees and the dancing teenagers inspired Marks to write "Rockin' Around the Christmas Tree".

Marks later went to a record company with his song and suggested that Brenda Lee (b.1944), a popular singer during that period, might record it. The record company executive was initially reluctant to honor Marks' request, blurting out, "Johnny, every songwriter in the world is calling me about a song for Brenda. But you, of all people! You don't even write rock music!" Eventually the record executive relented, and "Rockin' Around the Christmas Tree", recorded in 1960, became one of the biggest hits of Brenda Lee's career, successfully climbing the *Top 100 Billboard Chart* for several Christmas seasons in the early 1960s.

Little Girl Looking Downstairs at a Christmas Party
cover of McCall's,
December 1964
Norman Rockwell (1894-1978)

Rockin' around the Christmas tree
At the Christmas party hop.
Mistletoe hung where you can see
Ev'ry couple tries to stop.

Rockin' around the Christmas tree,
Let the Christmas spirit ring.
Later we'll have some pumpkin pie,
And we'll do some caroling.

You will get a sentimental feeling
When you hear voices singing,
"Let's be jolly;
Deck the halls with boughs of holly."

Rockin' around the Christmas tree,
Have a happy holiday.
Ev'ryone dancing merrily
In the new old-fashioned way.

Recording Artists—
Gene Autry and The
Pinafores with orchestral
accompaniment

Words & Music—
Johnny Marks (1909-1985),
American songwriter
and music publisher

Another example of Johnny Marks' penchant to write wonderful secular holiday songs, "Rudolph the Red-Nosed Reindeer" became an immediate big seller in 1949 when Gene Autry (1907-1998), of motion picture and singing cowboy fame, first recorded it.

The genesis of the song was the year 1939 when the brother-in-law of Johnny Marks, Robert May, an advertising copywriter, developed the familiar figure of Rudolph the Red-Nosed Reindeer as part of a Christmas promotional campaign for his employer, Montgomery Ward, a national department store chain. With the cooperation of his friend Denver Gillen (b.1914), an illustrator for the chain store's art department, May created a colorful story that became an instant sensation. Children who came to visit Santa Claus at Montgomery Ward stores were given a free copy of the booklet, and for several years millions more of this eagerly sought item were dispensed in similar fashion. Unfortunately, due to a severe paper shortage during World War II, Montgomery Ward's Christmas give-away program had to stop. Robert May eventually acquired the rights to Rudolph from his employer, and in 1947 he published the first hardback edition of the story.

When Johnny Marks wrote the first draft of the song, he thought it was the worst song he had ever composed. About a year later, while walking in Greenwich Village in New York, he finally solved a musical obstacle he had had with

Santa Enlisting Rudolph the
Red-Nosed Reindeer
1939 booklet illustration
Denver Laredo Gillen (b.1914)

the initial draft. Marks then sent a demo of his new song to Gene Autry as a possibility for his next recording session. But Autry ruled it out, saying he felt that it didn't fit his cowboy image. However, Autry's wife, Ina Mae, who was enthusiastic about the song, asked her husband to record it as a favor to her. "Put it on the 'B' side," she said, "and put whatever you want on the 'A' side." Autry took his wife's advice, and, as luck would have it, the song became the biggest hit of his career and in the history of Columbia Records.

Other notable achievements for "Rudolph the Red-Nosed Reindeer" include the following: 1) selected for the Hall of Fame of the National Academy of Arts & Sciences (sponsors of the Grammy Awards); 2) ranked in the *Top 100 Most-Recorded Songs* since 1890; and 3) considered one of the most valuable songs in the world, having sold more than 170,000,000 copies.

Rudolph Joining the Other Reindeer
1939 booklet illustration
Denver Laredo Gillen (b.1914)

You know Dasher and Dancer
and Prancer and Vixen,
Comet and Cupid and Donner and Blitzen,
But do you recall
The most famous reindeer of all?

Rudolph the Red-Nosed Reindeer
Had a very shiny nose,
And if you ever saw it,
You would even say it glows.

All of the other reindeer
Used to laugh and call him names;
They never let poor Rudolph
Join in any reindeer games.

Then one foggy Christmas Eve
Santa came to say:
"Rudolph with your nose so bright,
Won't you guide my sleigh tonight?"

Then how the reindeer loved him,
As they shouted out with glee,
"Rudolph the Red-Nosed Reindeer,
You'll go down in history."

33 *Santa Claus Is Comin' to Town*

Recording Artist —
Willie Nelson

Words —
Haven Gillespie
(1888-1975),
American songwriter

Music —
John Frederick Coots
(1897-1985), American
pianist and songwriter

The modern image of a jolly Santa Claus was embellished by Thomas Nast (1840-1902), a noted German-born American illustrator and political cartoonist, about fifty years after Clement Clark Moore's poem "A Visit from St. Nicholas" (also known as "'Twas the Night Before Christmas") was first published. Nast, known also for creating the political symbols of an elephant for the Republican Party and a donkey for the Democratic Party, was rather fond of Santa Claus and stories about him. He went on to create a number of Santa Claus illustrations for *The Harper's Weekly*, a periodical with which he enjoyed a long association, first on a free-lance basis and then as a regular from 1862, the height of the Civil War, until 1888. After that, Nast started his own newspaper, and though it failed, he continued to make Santa Claus illustrations. It is probable that Nast's Santa Claus served as the model for the familiar rosy-cheek Santa of the 20th century.

Although "Santa Claus Is Comin' to Town" was composed in 1932 by Haven Gillespie and John Frederick Coots, the song did not receive immediate attention. But two years later at Thanksgiving time, Ida Cantor persuaded her husband, Eddie Cantor (1892-1964), to give the song a chance on his popular national radio program. The song became an immediate success. George Hall and

Caught!
from Harper's Weekly,
December 24, 1881
Thomas Nast (1840-1902)

Children on Christmas
Morning with RCA Radio
c.1935 oil on canvas
Roy Spreter (1899-1967)

his Orchestra, with vocalist Sonny Schuyler, released it as a recording, and it rose
to the number-twelve spot on pop music charts during the 1934 Christmas season. In 1947 Bing Crosby and the Andrews Sisters also enjoyed a successful recording of the song. Ranked in the *Top 100 Most-Recorded Songs* in the history of modern music, "Santa Claus Is Comin' to Town" is one of the season's more memorable tunes and continues to bring listening pleasure to children and parents alike.

> Oh, you better watch out; you better not cry;
> You better not pout; I'm telling you why:
> Santa Claus is comin' to town.
> He's making a list and checking it twice;
> Gonna find out who's naughty and nice:
> Santa Claus is comin' to town.
>
> He sees you when you're sleepin';
> He knows when you're awake;
> He knows if you've been bad or good;
> So be good for goodness sake.
> Oh, you better watch out; you better not cry;
> You better not pout; I'm telling you why:
> Santa Claus is comin' to town.

34 ❋ The Shepherd's Carol

Other Title—
Boston & Shiloh

Recording Artist—
Catherdral Choir of
St. John the Divine

Words & Music—
William Billings
(1746-1800), American
composer and music teacher

William Billings was one of the most prolific composers in America during the Revolutionary War era. He was a self-taught individual who did not enjoy the benefit of a formal education, largely because his father had died when he was only fourteen. In addition, Billings eschewed the dogmatic standards set by the music establishment of the day, one largely influenced by European composers. His independent musical style was often intertwined with a vigorous musical idiom commonly found in the English country parish church. He even used dissonance on rare occasions as a creative technique, one that would not find favor in Europe until the first half of the 20th century with the music of Charles Ives (1874-1954), another independent-minded American composer. Billings wrote many hymns, psalms, and anthems during his life, but he died in poverty in the city of Boston because his musical contributions were not protected by copyright.

"The Shepherd's Carol", an attractive composition whose text had dramatic roles for the first shepherd and first angel as part of the narrative, was a fusion of the lyrics from the hymns "Boston" and "Shiloh". Although these hymns reflected Billings' musical style and spirituality, their tone was still puritanical, slightly more strict than merry, and in a style more suited to Pentecostal themes. One must remember that the Puritans, particularly those of New England, had

gone so far as to abolish the celebration of Christmas in the 17th century, and their descendants continued to discourage it in the 18th and 19th centuries because they considered Christmas a minor holiday. Though the lyrics of "The Shepherd's Carol", published in *The Singing Master's Assistant*, a 1786 Boston hymn book, seem rather quaint, there is no mistaking the earnestness of the Nativity message.

Methinks I see an heav'nly Host
Of Angels on the Wing;
Methinks I hear their cheerful Notes,
So merrily they Sing.

Let all your fears be banished hence,
Glad tidings I proclaim;
For there's a Savior born today,
And Jesus is his Name.

Lay down your Crooks and quit your flocks,
To Bethlehem repair;
And let your wandering steps be squar'd
By yonder shining Star.

Seek not in Courts or Palaces,
Nor Royal curtains draw;
But search the Stable, see your God
Extended on the Straw.

Then learn from hence, ye mortal swains,
The meekness of your God,
Who left the boundless Realms of Joy,
To Ransom you with Blood.

The master of the inn refused
A more commodius place;
Ungen'rous soul of savage mould,
And destitute of Grace.

Exult ye Oxen, low for Joy,
Ye tenants of the Stall,
Pay your obeisance, on your knees
Unanimously fall.

The Royal Guest you entertain
Is not of common Birth,
But second to the Great I Am;
The God of Heav'n and Earth.

Then suddenly a Heav'nly Host
Around the Shepherds throng,
Exulting in the threefold God
And thus address their Song.

To God the Father, Christ the Son,
And Holy Ghost ador'd;
The first and last, the last and first,
Eternal Praise afford.

35 *The Shepherd's Story*

Recording Artists—
Mormon Tabernacle Choir/
Alexander Schriener &
Frank Asper, organ

Words—
William Morris
(1834-1896), English
poet, painter, and inventor

Music—
Clarence Dickinson
(1873-1969), American
composer and organist

A carol with both American and English roots and dating from the late 19th century and early 20th century, "The Shepherd's Story" is quite interesting due to its peculiar rhythm and unusual phrasing. This sacred account of the shepherds going to Bethlehem to visit the newborn Christ Child seems to closely resemble that of "Masters in This Hall", although the lyrics of the latter were based initially on secular carols sung in the drinking halls of olden England.

The lyrics for "The Shepherd's Story" were written by William Morris, an accomplished poet who also was well respected as both a designer and painter of stained glass windows, a number of which grace churches and cathedrals in England and the United States. Clarence Dickinson, an American organist, probably composed the music for the carol around 1913.

The world-renowned Mormon Tabernacle Choir, in a glorious and reverential musical style, provokes a sense of awe as though guiding us to a brilliant star that once had bestowed favor on poor shepherds tending their sheep on the hills of Bethlehem.

Nowell! Nowell! Nowell! Nowell! Nowell!
Sing we clear! Holpen are all folk on earth,
Born is God's Son so dear.

Angels Appearing Before the Shepherds, *1901*
Henry Ossawa Tanner
(1859-1937), African-American
National Museum of American
Art, Smithsonian Institution

Annunciation to the Shepherds
1864 stained glass panel
Edward Burne-Jones (1833-1898),
English

To Bethlem did they go, the Shepherds go;
(The Shepherds three to Bethlem did they go),
To Bethlem did they go, to see whe'r it were so or no,
Whether Christ were born or no to set men free.

Masters, in this hall, hear ye news today
Brought over sea, and ever you I pray.

Nowell! Nowell! Nowell! Nowell! Nowell!
Sing we clear! Holpen are all folk on earth,
Born is God's Son so dear.

Then to Bethlem town did the Shepherds go,
And in a sorry place heard the oxen low.
Therein did they see a sweet and goodly May
(And a fair old man)
Upon the straw she lay.

And a little child on her arm had she
"Wot ye who this is?" said the hinds to me.
Ox and ass him know kneeling on their knee:
Wondrous joy had I this little Babe to see.

Nowell! Nowell! Nowell!
This is Christ the Lord, Masters, be ye glad!
Christmas is come in, and no folk should be sad.

Nowell! Nowell! Nowell! Nowell! Nowell!
Sing we clear! Holpen are all folk on earth,
Born is God's Son so dear.

36 ❄ *Silver Bells*

Recording Artists—
Mormon Tabernacle Choir/
The Columbia Symphony
Orchestra;
Jerold Ottley, director

Words—
Ray Evans (b.1915),
American songwriter

Music—
Jay Livingston
(b.1915), American
composer and pianist

"Silver Bells" has the distinction of being one of the first holiday songs about Christmas in the city. At the time of its creation in 1951, most Christmas songs celebrated the warmth associated with country settings. The song's composers, Ray Evans and Jay Livingston, were assigned by the producers of Paramount Pictures to write it for the movie *The Lemon Drop Kid*, starring the irrepressible Bob Hope (b.1903) and Marilyn Maxwell (1922-1972). Evans and Livingston at first were reluctant because they thought there was little chance a new Christmas song would be successful when so many Christmas songs were already being sung by the American public. Eventually the two wrote about Santa Claus and the bell-ringing Salvation Army volunteers who worked the city sidewalks populated by busy shoppers during the holiday season.

The song, boosted to popularity by Bing Crosby (1903-1977), probably the most famous American male singer of the 1930s and 1940s, has become one of several classics composed during the 1940-1954 heyday of American holiday song composition. Although the introductory stanza is generally omitted in most versions, there is no denying the 1950s flavor of the Christmas spirit that permeates the song. Perhaps this is the result of the composers' effort to write the verse and chorus so that they could be sung simultaneously.

Livingston would collaborate again with Evans to write "Que Sera, Sera," for the 1956 Alfred Hitchcock movie thriller *The Man Who Knew Too Much*. In addition, he worked with a number of other well-known composers during his ca-

Christmas Time in the City
illustration from LIFE,
December 20, 1948
John Gannam (1905-1965)

reer, writing many film themes and title songs. Two of his songs won an Academy Award for Best Song: "Buttons and Bows" in 1948 and "Mona Lisa" in 1950. Four other songs were Academy nominations, including "Almost in Your Arms", "The Cat and the Canary", "Tammy", and "Dear Heart". Familiar television themes from popular shows such as *Bonanza*, *Mister Ed*, and *Mr. Lucky* were products of his fertile musical imagination.

For Livingston and Evans, "Silver Bells" is their signature holiday song. When it is played each season, we might remember a child's thrill of going downtown to gaze at huge department store windows so richly decorated with holiday wreaths and ornaments. Or we might recall, in an admiring fashion, the large Christmas tree in a city square, or just mingling with the busy sidewalk crowds of shoppers and other children, many of them with holiday smiles, when we were smitten with that wonderful feeling of Christmas. Who can forget such sweetness when the magical sounds of "Silver Bells" fill the air?

Christmas makes you feel emotional.
It may bring parties or thoughts devotional.
Whatever happens or what may be,
Here is what Christmas means to me.

City sidewalks, busy sidewalks,
Dressed in holiday style.
In the air there's a feeling of Christmas.
Children laughing, people passing,
Meeting smile after smile,
And on ev'ry street corner you hear:
Silver bells, silver bells,
It's Christmas time in the city.
Ring-a-ling, hear them ring,
Soon it will be Christmas day.

Strings of street lights, even stop lights,
Blink a bright red and green,
As the shoppers rush home with their treasures.
Hear the snow crunch, see the kids bunch,
This is Santa's big scene,
And above all this bustle you hear:
Silver bells, silver bells,
It's Christmas time in the city.
Ring-a-ling, hear them ring,
Soon it will be Christmas day.

Recording Artist—
Mormon Tabernacle Choir/
The Columbia Symphony
Orchestra;
Jerold Ottley, director

Words—
Mitchell Parish
(1900-1993), American
songwriter and performer
for stage and screen

Music—
Leroy Anderson
(1908-1975), American
composer, arranger, and
conductor

In 1950 Mitchell Parish added the words to this originally instrumental piece by Leroy Anderson. Anderson composed the brilliant music in 1948, perhaps gaining inspiration by listening to Mozart's work of the same title. Both Parish and Anderson were noted for other popular works. Parish was responsible for the lyrics of the wistful and beautiful "Stardust", "Moonlight Serenade", and "Stairway to the Stars". Anderson, who also served as an arranger for the Boston Pops Orchestra, composed an interesting variety of unusual but well-crafted works, including "The Syncopated Clock", "Fiddle Faddle", "Bugler's Holiday", "The Typewriter", "Serenata", and "Blue Tango".

As an instrumental piece, the light-hearted classic "Sleigh Ride" incorporates bells, horse whinnies, and whip cracking—sound effects that help to develop a picturesque setting of a snowy countryside and sleigh riding. The wonderful imagery of wintry holiday scenes, also captured by the vocal rendition of the renowned Mormon Tabernacle Choir, commonly adorned the prized lithographs of Currier & Ives in the mid-to-late 19th century.

Just hear those sleigh bells jingling, ring ting tingling too;
Come on, it's lovely weather for a sleigh ride together with you.
Outside, the snow is falling and friends are calling "Yoo-hoo";
Come on, it's lovely weather for a sleigh ride together with you.

Giddy-yap, giddy-yap, giddy-yap, let's go;
Let's look at the show;
We're riding in a wonderland of snow.
Giddy-yap, giddy-yap, giddy-yap it's grand,

Early Winter, *1869*
"Currier & Ives" lithograph
The Museum of the City of New York

Just holding your hand;
We're gliding along with a song of a wintery fairyland.

Our cheeks are nice and rosy, and comfy cozy are we;
We're snuggled up together like two birds of a feather would be.
Let's take that road before us and sing a chorus or two;
Come on, it's lovely weather for a sleigh ride together with you.

There's a birthday party at the home of farmer Gray;
It'll be a perfect ending of a perfect day.
We'll be singing the songs we love to sing without a single stop,
At the fireplace while we watch the chestnuts pop, pop, pop, pop.

There's a happy feeling nothing in the world can buy,
When they pass around the cider and the pumpkin pie,
It'll nearly be like a picture print by Currier and Ives.
These wonderful things are the things we remember all thru' our lives.

Just hear those sleigh bells jingling, ring ting tingling too;
Come on, it's lovely weather for a sleigh ride together with you.
Outside, the snow is falling and friends are calling "Yoo-hoo";
Come on, it's lovely weather for a sleigh ride together with you.

Giddy-yap, giddy-yap, giddy-yap, let's go;
Let's look at the show;
We're riding in a wonderland of snow.
Giddy-yap, giddy-yap, giddy-yap it's grand,
Just holding your hand;
We're gliding along with a song of a wintery fairyland.

Our cheeks are nice and rosy and comfy cozy are we;
We're snuggled up together like two birds of a feather would be.
Let's take the road before us and sing a chorus or two;
Come on, it's lovely weather for a sleigh ride together with you.

38 *Some Children See Him*

Recording Artist—
Andy Williams;
Arranged & conducted
by Robert Mersey

Words—
Wihla Hutson
(b.1901), American church
organist and composer

Music—
Alfred Burt
(1920-1954), American
composer, singer, and
trumpeter

The lyrics of "Some Children See Him" were written by Wihla Hutson, a close friend of Alfred Burt and his father, the Rev. Bates Burt (1878-1948). She was a church organist in Michigan for more than 50 years. Alfred composed the music to the carol in 1951, and it was one of fifteen carols he had composed as Christmas card gifts, a practice begun by his father in 1926 for friends of the family.

This delightful practice came easy to the Burts, a close-knit group whose members were all musically inclined. The Rev. Bates Burt, a self-taught musician, had a keen interest in music for the church, and he introduced his family to the classics. His youngest son, Alfred, composed music at an early age and had an affinity for the trumpet. Alfred's first musical instrument, in fact, was a "silver trumpet" that he received when he refused to go into the hospital for an appendectomy unless he was rewarded. Thus, began Alfred's musical journey in life. He excelled in school and college and won a Fellowship for Music Theory at the University of Michigan that he could not use due to his induction into the Army Air Force. When he was not playing first trumpet, his love of music included writing arrangements for the orchestra, often at the family dinner table, and just as often for modern music and jazz for various bands before and after his four-year-stint with the military.

Christmas had always meant a great deal to the Burts, both as a Church festival and a time for family gathering. The Rev. Bates Burt had always written the carol words for his family's annual Christmas card. But after his death in 1948, Alfred and his wife continued the family tradition of composing carols as personal Christmas cards (a list that grew from 50 to 450 as they toured from city to city) and Wihla Hutson was asked to be the lyricist. For many years Hutson had written verses for the family, especially at Christmas time when they were placed in Christmas stockings. Since Alfred and his wife were on the road a lot due to the demands of concert tours, Hutson often had to mail them the new carol verses, and soon after receiving them Alfred wrote the music.

In the early 1950s, the carol compositions of Alfred Burt and Wihla Hutson were sung at various public and church concerts. However, by the summer of 1954, when new carols were being composed, the still young Alfred had become gravely ill. A good friend, who was also the choir director at the Episcopal church where Alfred worshipped, arranged to have them recorded. Knowing his time was short, Burt worked on the unfinished carols, completing them just before his death. It was a great moment for him when he heard them recorded and sung by a volunteer chorus. The knowledge that Columbia Records had decided to release the recordings did a lot to ease his suffering before he died.

With strong contributions by Wihla Hutson, Alfred Burt left behind a carol legacy of joy and eternal hope, just as his father had done before him. As a result, the Christmas story is uniquely related in the tender "Some Children See

~ *111*

Him". What makes the carol even more endearing is that it honored racial diversity long before it had become politically fashionable in the United States. Note how the lyrics portray the innocent and unconditional love each child has toward another one born two thousand years ago. As seen through their eyes, love not only shines brightly as a soft steady flame, but also bears witness as the Christmas ideal.

Some Children See Him
c.1960
American Christmas card
Free Library of Philadelphia

Some children see Him lily white,
The Baby Jesus born this night.
Some children see Him lily white,
With tresses soft and fair.

Some children see Him bronzed and brown,
The Lord of heav'n to earth come down;
Some children see Him bronzed and brown,
With dark and heavy hair.

Some children see Him almond eyed,
This Saviour whom we kneel beside,
Some children see Him almond eyed,
With skin of yellow hue.

Some children see Him dark as they,
Sweet Mary's Son to whom we pray;
Some children see Him dark as they,
And ah! they love Him, too!

The children in each diff'rent place
Will see the Baby Jesus' face
Like theirs, but bright with heav'nly grace
And filled with holy light.

O lay aside each earthly thing,
And with thy heart as offering,
Come worship now the Infant King,
'Tis love that's born tonight!

39 *The Star Carol*

Recording Artist—
"Tennessee" Ernie Ford

Words—
*Wihla Hutson
(b.1901), American
church organist and
composer*

Music—
*Alfred Burt
(1920-1954), American
composer, singer, and
trumpeter*

The Nativity Star, c.1950
*Lauren Ford (1893-1973)
Private Collection*

"The Star Carol" is another collaborative effort by Wihla Hutson and Alfred Burt to produce a carol Christmas card. Composed in 1948, possibly at the invitation of the Rev. Bates Burt (1878-1948), the father of Alfred Burt, "The Star Carol" was eventually published and released as a recording in 1954.

Hutson, a close friend of the Burt family for many years, worked for the Episcopal Diocese of Michigan for 44 years and as a church organist for 50 years. She was quite fond of church music and composed anthems, organ pieces, and several choral numbers. But she was most noted for her association with the Burt family and her lyrical compositions of their family Christmas cards.

Her heart-warming lyrics were a trademark of a simple poetic style, one that shared a kinship with the humble carols that were created in 15th- and 16th-century England. "The Star Carol" is a special tribute to Hutson's ability to raise simplicity to soaring heights. Notice how her lyrics herald the birth of Christ and bring luster to it with the appearance of a bright star and heavenly angels over the town of Bethlehem.

"Tennessee" Ernie Ford (1919-1991), a popular country and noted gospel singer blessed with a rich baritone voice, and a former television host and entertainer, further enriches the carol's lyrics with a great depth of feeling.

Long years ago on a deep winter night,
High in the heav'ns a star shone bright,
While in a manger a wee Baby lay,
Sweetly asleep on a bed of hay.

Jesus, the Lord was that Baby so small,
Laid down to sleep in a humble stall;
Then came the star and it stood overhead,
Shedding its light 'round His little bed.

Dear Baby Jesus, how tiny Thou art,
I'll make a place for Thee in my heart,
And when the stars in the heavens I see,
Ever and always I think of Thee.

40 Star in the East

Other Title—
Brightest and Best

Recording Artist—
The Western Wind Singers

Words & Music—
Anonymous early 19th century American folk

"Star in the East" is the product of native singing schools on the frontiers of the southern and western United States that were particularly prominent in their influence during the 18th and 19th centuries. The carol emphasizes the tradition of the holy birth and how a bright star leads the shepherds to a manger in Bethlehem. The lyrics are similar to those of an English carol titled "Brightest and Best", but the music exhibits a rugged individuality typical of the folk composers of the American frontiers while still providing a reverential tone and cadence for the simple folk lyrics.

The phenomenon of the Star of Bethlehem, or star in the east, was noticed by the Magi according to Matthew, one of the two authors of the Christmas Gospels. There may have been a planetary conjunction involving Mars, Jupiter, and Saturn around December in 7 B.C., an event that may have accounted for what the Magi had witnessed. Such a conjunction would have created a brilliant shining which would have been particularly evident to astronomers, or Wise Men. In 1604, the great German astronomer Johannes Kepler (1571-1630) calculated that this rare conjunction would occur every 805 years.

Another planetary conjunction is thought to have resulted in the appearance of the Star of Bethlehem. When the planets Jupiter, Venus, and Mars closely converged in 2 B.C., that event might have been seen by the Magi near Babylon as they set out to travel in the direction of Palestine. What makes this plausible is that the exact date of Christ's birth is not known. Another convergence of Jupiter, Venus, and Mars occurred as recently as June 16-23, 1991, especially on the night of June 17th when Venus passed Jupiter. Regardless of which scientific explanation accurately portrays the exciting phenomenon of the shining star, the simple splendor of such an event shines through the lyrics of this folk carol.

Hail the blest morn; see the great Mediator
Down from the regions of glory descends!
Shepherds, go worship the babe in the manger;
Lo, for his guard the bright angels attend.
    REFRAIN:
    Brightest , and best of the sons of the morning,
    Dawn on our darkness, and lend us thine aid!
    Star in the East, the horizon adorning.
    Guide where our infant Redeemer was laid.

Cold on his cradle the dewdrops are shining;
Low lies his bed with the beasts of the stall;
Angels adore him, in slumbers reclining,
Wise men and angels before him do fall.
    REFRAIN:

The Star of Bethlehem
oil on canvas
Elihu Vedder (1836-1923)
Speed Art Museum

Say, shall we yield Him in costly devotion,
Odours of Edom and offerings divine;
Gems of the mountain, and pearls of the ocean,
Myrrh from the forest, and gold from the mine.
    REFRAIN:

Vainly we offer each ample oblation,
Vainly with gold would his favour secure;
Richer by far is the heart's adoration,
Dearer to God are the prayers of the poor.
    REFRAIN:

Recording Artists—
Perry Como with the
Ray Charles Singers;
Arranged & conducted
by Nick Perito

Words—
Carl Sigman
(1909-2000), American
songwriter and composer

Music—
Mickey J. Addy (1894-?),
American composer

Another wonderful post-World War II holiday song, "There Is No Christmas Like a Home Christmas" was the product of an effort by Carl Sigman and Mickey Addy. Sigman, who was known by several names, wrote the musical scores for a number of shows and movies, including "Dream Along With Me", Perry Como's television theme song, and the theme song for the 1950s Robin Hood television series. Sigman was also noted for writing the lyrics and/or music for such popular songs as "Ebb Tide", "Arrivederci, Roma", "Pennsylvania 6-5000", "My Heart Cries for You", "Dance, Ballerina, Dance", the theme for "Where Do I Begin", "What Now My Love", and "A Marshmallow World".

Composed in 1950, a year noted for a number of newly introduced Christmas songs that would become seasonal standards, "There Is No Christmas Like a Home Christmas" resonates with the Christmas spirit characteristic of sharing special moments with mom and dad and the family at home for the Christmas holidays. Sigman's lyrics reinforce the quaint notion that all roads do indeed lead home during that very special time of the year.

Christmas Homecoming
cover of The Saturday
Evening Post
December 25, 1948
Norman Rockwell (1894-1978)

Christmas at Home, *1946*
oil on pressed wood
Grandma Moses (1860-1961)
Grandma Moses Properties

There is no Christmas like a home Christmas
With your Dad and Mother, Sis and Brother there,
With your hearts humming at your homecoming,
And the merry yuletide spirit in the air.
Christmas bells, Christmas bells,
Ringing loud and strong,
Follow them, follow them,
You've been away too long.

There is no Christmas like a home Christmas,
For that's the time of year all roads lead home.
Christmas bells, Christmas bells,
Ringing loud and strong,
Follow them, follow them,
You've been away too long.

There is no Christmas like a home Christmas,
For that's the time of year all roads lead home.

"Toyland" comes from the famous Victor Herbert operetta *Babes in Toyland*. First performed in Chicago on June 17, 1903, Herbert's production was immediately successful with the audience, which loved his music, the fancy costumes, and the creative scenery. Glen MacDonough wrote the lyrics for all of the songs of the show, except the masterful instrumental "March of the Toys", and he also wrote the libretto, i.e., the text of the operetta. A recording of "Toyland" was made by Corrine Morgan & the Haydn Quartet in 1904 and became the number-one song on the popular music charts.

Herbert enjoyed a successful career as a composer of light music. But success did not come readily to him. He studied cello in his early years and played the instrument in Eduard Strauss's waltz band in Vienna in 1880. He came to New York only because he had married a famous Viennese opera singer, Therese Forster (1861-1927), who was offered a starring role in a New York Metropolitan Opera production in 1886. In 1894 he wrote his first light opera. Ten years later he formed the Victor Herbert New York Orchestra.

Herbert, one of the founders of The American Society of Composers, Authors, and Publishers (ASCAP), the songwriters' association, intended *Babes in Toyland* primarily as an amusement for children. The spirit of Herbert's design has been kept intact by the inclusion of the nostalgic classic "Toyland" in Christmas song collections over the years.

Recording Artists—
Perry Como with the Ray
Charles Singers;
Arranged & conducted by
Nick Perito

Words—
Glen MacDonough
(1870-1924),
American songwriter

Music—
Victor Herbert (1859-1924),
Irish-born American
composer, conductor, and
cellist

Above:
"Babes in Toy Land"
1903 sheet music cover
National Museum of American
History, Smithsonian Institution

Right:
Child Playing with Toys
cover of The Saturday
Evening Post
December 25, 1909
Sarah Stilwell Weber
(1878-1939)

Toyland, Toyland,
Little girl and boy land.
While you dwell within it,
You are ever happy then.
Childhood's joyland,
Mystic, merry Toyland!
Once you pass its borders
You can ne'er return again.

43 ⁂ 'Twas the Night Before Christmas

Other Title—
The Night Before Christmas
Song

Recording Artists—
Fred Waring &
the Pennsylvanians

Words—
Clement Clarke Moore
(1779-1863), American
author, poet, and scholar;
adapted by Ken Darby

Music—
Ken Darby (1909-1992),
American composer
for film and television

"'Twas the Night Before Christmas" is a holiday song based on the famous poem, "A Visit from St. Nicholas", composed in 1822 by Clement Clarke Moore. The poem was first published anonymously in the *Troy Sentinel* of New York on December 23, 1823, and it quickly caught the fancy of the American public, although over the years it would become better known by its first line.

Ken Darby adopted this first line in 1942 as the title for his own musical interpretation of the poem. Darby, a gifted composer, also created Oscar Award-wining musical scores for several movies, including *The King and I, Camelot,* and *Porgy and Bess.* Other variant tunes of "'Twas the Night Before Christmas" were composed in 1951 by Frank Henri Klickman (1885-1966) and a year later by Johnny Marks (1909-1985), both American songwriters. Harry Simeone (b.1911), another American composer, provided the wonderful setting for Ken Darby's version. On balance the song is a delightful re-enactment of Moore's classic children's Christmas poem with a whimsical addition to the original text.

St. Nicholas, the main character of Clement Moore's poem, has been closely

St. Nicholas (golden balls represent dowries), *1425*
Gentile da Fabriano
(c.1370-1427), Florentine
Galleria degli Uffizi

St. Nicholas Resuscitating
the Three Youths
*(predella from altarpiece at
monastery of San Niccolo in
Caraggio)*
*Lorenzo Bicci (1371-1452),
Florentine, Metropolitan
Museum of Art, New York*

identified with Santa Claus. He was the Bishop of Myra around 300 A.D. in a province of Asia Minor called Lycia (in present-day Turkey). Born into a wealthy Christian family, St. Nicholas became a priest in the early Christian church and suffered persecution and imprisonment during the reign of the Emperor Diocletian (245-313 A.D.). He was noted for his holiness and hard work among the poor, giving them much of the wealth he had inherited from his father.

There are a number of legends about his good deeds. A neighbor's daughter, who did not have a dowry for marriage, would have been sold into slavery or prostitution were it not for his kind intervention. At the time it was normal to wash and hang stockings at night, either by a fireplace or a window. St. Nicholas wrapped gold in a handkerchief and dropped it through his neighbor's window and safely into the daughter's hung stocking, sparing her a life of ignominy. The custom of putting gifts in children's stockings supposedly is based on this legendary event.

Another legend has St. Nicholas performing a miracle, one that has earned him the hallowed title Patron Saint of Children. It involved three young students who were kidnapped, robbed, and dismembered by an evil innkeeper who then stuck their remains into empty pickle barrels. St. Nicholas suddenly appeared at the inn and commanded the boys to rise from the barrels. Piece by piece, all three boys were miraculously reassembled and brought back to life.

St. Nicholas was an extraordinarily popular saint of the Middle Ages. Indeed, he was the third most venerated figure in Christianity after Jesus Christ and the Virgin Mary. When he died, his body was revered and sought after for relics by the entire Christian world. Another legend of St. Nicholas started around 1087 when his relics were removed to Bari, Italy, for the purpose of helping sailors at sea. Besides being known as the Patron Saint of Children, especially sick ones whom he had brought back to health, and sailors, he is the patron of choir boys, prisoners, pawnbrokers (for putting gold in the daughter's stocking), and a host of other groups and causes. Inspired by his protection of children and miracles, French nuns in the 12th century began distributing candy on St. Nicholas Day, celebrated on December 6th. Eventually St. Nicholas himself was claimed to have come along and put candy in the shoes of good children. More than 2,000 churches are named in his honor worldwide, including 400 in England. In Greece and Russia he is even more venerated as each country's national saint.

St. Nicholas became known as "Father Christmas" during the Protestant Reformation in several European countries. In France he is celebrated as *Pere Noel*. In Italy the story of Befana, who leaves gifts for good children as she searches each house for the Christ Child, is based on his good deeds. He is especially admired in the Netherlands. In fact, Dutch settlers in New Amsterdam (known today as New York) brought with them their traditions of "Sinter Claes", or St. Nicholas, which would eventually spread in children's lore throughout the United States and the world.

Clement Moore, a noted scholar of Greek and English, unknowingly propagated the legend of the generous St. Nicholas when he wrote a simple Christmas poem for his children. His humorous description of a "jolly old elf", however, would undergo significant changes during the 19th and 20th centuries. Today we know Santa Claus, especially as popularized by The Coca-Cola Company, as a

St. Nicholas Gifts
Jan Steen (1626-1679), Dutch
Rijksmuseum, Amsterdam

much larger jolly old man with a glorious white beard, and rosy red cheeks, and dressed in a red fur-trimmed coat.

'Twas the night before Christmas,
And all through the house,
Not a creature was stirring,
Not even a mouse;
The stockings were hung by the chimney with care,
In hopes that St. Nicholas
Soon would be there.
The children were nestled
All snug in their wee little beds,
While visions of sugar-plums
Danced through their wee little heads.
Mama in her 'kerchief
And I in my cap,
Had just settled down
For a long winter's nap,
When out on the lawn
There arose such a clatter,
I sprang from my bed
To see what was the matter.
Away to the window
I flew like a flash,
Tore open the shutters,
Threw up the sash.
Then, what to my wondering
Eyes should appear,
But a miniature sleigh
And eight tiny reindeer,
With a little old driver,
So lively and quick,
That I knew right away
That it must be St. Nick.
More rapid than eagles
His coursers they came,
And he whistled and shouted
And called them by name:
"Now Dasher! Now, Dancer!
Now, Prancer and Vixen!
On, Comet! On, Cupid!
On, Donner and Blitzen!

A Right Jolly Old Elf with a Stump of a Little Old Pipe
engraving from 1848 publication
"A Visit from St. Nicholas"
*Theodore C. Boyd
(19th century)*

To the top of the porch,
To the top of the wall!
Dash away, dash away,
Dash away, dash away all!"
So, up to the house-tops
The coursers they flew,
With a sleigh full of toys,
And St. Nicholas, too.
And then in a twinkling
I heard on the roof
All the clattering noise
Of each galloping hoof.
All bundled in fur,
From his head to his foot;
His clothes were all tarnished
With ashes and soot.
I drew in my head
And was turning around,
When down the chimney
He came with a bound!
A bag full of toys
He had flung on his back,
And he looked like
A little old peddler
Just op'ning his pack.
His eyes how they twinkled so gay!
His cheeks were like roses,
When kissed by the sun!
His droll little mouth
Was drawn up like a bow!
The beard on his chin
Was as white as the snow.
The stump of a little old pipe
He held tight in his teeth,
And the smoke went around,
And around, and around
His head like a wreath.
He was so jolly and plump,
A right jolly old, jolly old elf.
And I laughed, and I laughed,
And I laughed when I saw him
In spite of myself.

"Merry Old Santa Claus"
from Harper's Weekly
January 1, 1888
Thomas Nast (1840-1902)

Good Boys and Girls
1951 Coca-Cola advertisement
Haddon H. Sundblom
(1899-1976)

Facing page:
The Three Wise Men
c.1878 oil on canvas
John La Farge (1835-1910)
Museum of Fine Art, Boston

He had a broad face, Ho! Ho! Ho!,
And a little round belly, Hee! Hee! Hee!
That shook when he laughed, Ho! Ho! Ho!
Like a bowl full of jelly, Hah! Hah! Hah!
He gave me a wink of his eye
And a twist of his head
A chuckle and a smile
I knew all the while
I had nothing to dread.
He spoke not a word,
But went straight to his work.
He filled all the stockings,
Then turned with a jerk,
And laying a finger
Aside of his nose,
And giving a nod,
Up the chimney he rose.
He sprang to his sleigh
To his team gave a whistle,
And away they all flew
Like the down of a thistle;
But I heard him exclaim,
Ere he drove out of sight:
"Merry Christmas to all,
And to all goodnight."

'Tis the night after Christmas,
And all through the house,
Not a creature is stirring,
Not even a mouse.
The presents are scattered
And broken I fear,
And St. Nicholas won't come
Again for a year.
The children are nestled
All snug in their wee little beds,
While mem'ries of sugar-plums
Dance in their wee little heads.
Mama in her 'kerchief,
Papa in his cap,
Are settled at last
For a long winter's nap.

We Three Kings of Orient Are

Recording Artists—
Robert Shaw Chamber
Singers/Ronald Burrichter,
tenor; Victor Ledbetter,
baritone;
Wayne Baughman, bass

Words & Music—
John Henry Hopkins
(1820-1891), American
minister, composer, music
teacher, and designer
of stained glass windows

"We Three Kings of Orient Are" is one of the few carols whose theme is primarily about the visit of the Kings, or Wise Men, to the Christ Child in Bethlehem. Written in 1857 by the Reverend John Henry Hopkins, "Kings of Orient", its original title, was later published in 1863 in his popular work *Carols, Hymns, and Songs*. It quickly gained recognition outside the United States, especially in England, where it was the only American carol published in *Christmas Carols, New and Old*, a landmark 1871 collection that was influential in the ongoing evolution of carol collecting and singing in England.

Hopkins wrote the carol as a Christmas gift for his nieces and nephews while he was in New York serving, among other things, as an instructor of church music for the General Theological Seminary there. Because the music has an archaic flavor, the carol is often thought to be older than it actually is. Plus, the unique

structure of Hopkins' carol allowed the kings to have direct speech and an opportunity for drama.

The journey of the Three Kings as Wise Men, or Magi, a class of priestly astrologers and magicians of Persia, appears in the *New Testament* in *St. Matthew 2:1-11*. Some suggestions about the Magi and the Star of Bethlehem came from the *Old Testament*, namely from *Psalms 68:29-31*; *Isaiah 49:7* and *60:3,6,10*; and *Numbers 24:17*.

During the early days of the Christian Church, the exotic story of the Three Kings caught the popular imagination, and the three acquired names: 1) Caspar (or Gaspar), the King of Tarsus; 2) Melchior, the King of Arabia and Nubia; and 3) Balthasar, the King of Saba (or Sheba). One of the first images of the three, depicting them as part of a crèche scene worshipping the Christ Child, appeared in the 4th century as a painting on a sarcophagus, now located in the Basilica of Saint Maximin, France. Since then they have continued to be so honored and have become a permanent part of Christmas lore.

An interesting custom has developed over the years regarding the Three Kings. Each year, after the heads of households have received their first Christmas card with a picture of the Three Kings on it, it is tacked over the front entrance of the house. This custom had its origins in Europe, where for centuries, on the day of the Epiphany, or January 6th, parish churches blessed and distributed water and chalk for the blessing of homes.

The water was used in remembrance of Baptism. The chalk was used to mark over the front door the initials of the Three Kings and the numerals of the new year, e.g., 19+C+M+B+99 (for the year 1999), or 20+C+M+B+00 (for the year 2000). From the greatest palaces to the humblest dwellings, the chalk marks were the same for all households. These markings were intended to lead the Three Kings, should they return, to easily find where Christ would be—in the hearts and minds of everyone.

Given the wealth of Christmas stories surrounding the Three Kings, it is understandable where Hopkins would have looked for his inspiration.

We three kings of Orient are,   (sung by *The Three Kings*)
Bearing gifts we traverse afar
Field and fountain, moor and mountain,
Following yonder star.
   REFRAIN:
   O Star of wonder, Star of might,
   Star with royal beauty bright,
   Westward leading, still proceeding,
   Guide us to Thy perfect light.

Born a King on Bethlehem's plain,   (sung by *Gaspar*)
Gold I bring to crown Him again;
King forever, ceasing never
Over us all to reign.
    REFRAIN:

Frankincense to offer have I,   (sung by *Melchior*)
Incense owns a Deity nigh;
Prayer and praising, all men raising,
Worship Him, God on high.
    REFRAIN:

Myrrh is mine; its bitter perfume   (sung by *Balthazar*)
Breathes a life of gathering gloom;
Sorrowing, sighing, bleeding, dying,
Sealed in the stone-cold tomb.
    REFRAIN:

Glorious now behold Him arise,   (sung by *All*)
King, and God, and Sacrifice;
Heav'n sings Alleluia;
Alleluia the earth replies.
    REFRAIN:

Recording Artist—
Johnny Mathis;
Arranged & conducted
by Ernie Freeman

Words & Music—
Frank Loesser
(1910-1969), American
composer, pianist, singer,
and newspaper reporter

Frank Loesser was a prolific composer of Broadway musical songs. He first earned his wings by writing songs for college shows and then later for Army shows during World War II. He won the Tony Award of his scores for *My Fair Lady*, *Camelot*, and *Gigi*. Some of his more notable popular songs include "I Go for That", "Heart and Soul", "Hey, Good Lookin'!", "Kiss the Boys Good-bye", "Jingle, Jangle, Jingle", "On a Slow Boat to China", "Luck Be a Lady", and "Baby, It's Cold Outside".

In 1947 he wrote "What Are You Doing New Year's Eve?", a melodious and somewhat sad lyric that contrasts sharply with most Christmas holiday songs. What seems evident in the text are palpable twinges of an unrequited love. Does this reflect apprehension not being able to spend a romantic New Year's Eve with a person loved from afar? Or is the song's melancholy tone the result of the holidays coming to an end? True to his more upbeat impulses, however, Loesser provides a kite of hope with the line "in case I stand one little chance". Johnny Mathis (b.1935), a popular African-American singer during the late 1950s and 1960s, endows us with a masterful interpretation of Frank Loesser's bittersweet song.

New Year's Eve
cover of The Saturday
Evening Post
January 3, 1948
John Falter (1910-1982)

Maybe it's much too early in the game,
Ah, but I thought I'd ask you just the same,
"What are you doing New Year's, New Year's Eve?"

Wonder whose arms will hold you good and tight,
When it's exactly twelve o'clock that night,
Welcoming in the New Year's, New Year's Eve.

Maybe I'm crazy to suppose
I'd ever be the one you chose
Out of the thousand invitations you'll receive.

Ah, but in case I stand one little chance,
Here comes the jackpot question in advance,
"What are you doing New Year's, New Year's Eve?"

46 White Christmas

Recording Artist—
Bing Crosby

Words & Music—
Irving Berlin
(1888-1989), American
songwriter, singer, and actor

Before he quietly fell asleep for the final time at the age of 101, Irving Berlin had written over 1,000 songs during his illustrious career. "God Bless America", "Easter Parade", "Alexander's Ragtime Band", and "Puttin' on the Ritz" are just a few of his songs that became big hits. Mostly happy and inspirational in tone, these songs were the trademarks of a Russian immigrant who truly loved America and all that she stood for. Berlin was one of America's finest songwriters of the 20th century.

His holiday song "White Christmas", which he believed was both the greatest song he ever wrote and the greatest song of all time, was written in 1940 dur-

White Christmas, *1954*
oil on pressed wood
Grandma Moses (1860-1961)
Grandma Moses Properties

ing the shooting of the film *Holiday Inn*. Some of Berlin's colleagues thought the song "seemed nice enough but no one thought it would be much else." However, Berlin believed the song would really make it big, and he was often found on the movie set trying not to be noticed as he peeked in on Bing Crosby (1904-1977), the famous American crooner and actor, when he was singing the song. Berlin was very pleased with the final results, but he would have to wait until August 1942 to find out how the public would react to "White Christmas". World War II was quite intense by that time, and the song easily became a nostalgic favorite for American soldiers abroad and their families at home.

"White Christmas" has since become one of the best-selling records of all time, making it also one of the most valuable songs ever written. Berlin's holiday song, which included introductory lyrics that were not sung by Bing Crosby, has won a number of awards, including an Academy Award for Best Song in 1942, recognition as the most-recorded secular holiday song of all time, ranked in the Top Ten for sales of sheet music songs, and election into the Hall of Fame of the National Academy of Recording Arts & Sciences, the Grammy Awards organization. In a nutshell, "White Christmas" is one of the holiday season's all-time classics!

> The sun is shining, the grass is green,
> The orange and palm trees sway.
> There's never been such a day in Beverly Hills, L.A.
> But it's December the twenty-fourth
> And I am longing to be up north.
>
> I'm dreaming of a white Christmas,
> just like the ones I used to know,
> where the treetops glisten and children listen
> to hear sleigh bells in the snow.
>
> I'm dreaming of a white Christmas
> with every Christmas card I write:
> May your days be merry and bright,
> and may all your Christmases be white!

47 ✻ Winter Wonderland

Recording Artists—
Johnny Mathis with Percy
Faith & His Orchestra

Words—
Richard B. Smith
(1901-1935),
American author

Music—
Felix Bernard (1897-1944),
American composer, pianist,
and conductor

Capturing the magic of a brisk winter day amid a snowy white panorama, "Winter Wonderland" has become one of the top Christmas holiday favorites in the United States. Both the song's romantic lyrics by Richard B. Smith and the bouncy music by Felix Bernard were written in 1934. Released the same year as a recording by Guy Lombardo and his Royal Canadians, a popular group that had sold more than 100 million records over the decades, "Winter Wonderland" quickly rose to the number-two spot on the popular music charts.

"Winter Wonderland", whose introductory stanza is seldom used, was popularized again in 1946 with separate record releases by the Andrews Sisters and Perry Como (1913-2000), both popular with the American public at that time. In 1947 the song rose to number four on the record sales charts when Johnny Mercer (1909-1976), a gifted songwriter who earned several Academy Awards for Best Song, released it. Since then, the special magic of "Winter Wonderland", much to the delight of the American public, has been captured many times over by succeeding generations of recording artists.

(Over the ground lies a mantle of white,
A heaven of diamonds shine down thru the night;
Two hearts are thrillin' in spite of the chill
In the weather.
Love knows no season; love knows no clime;
Romance can blossom any old time;
Here in the open, we're walkin'
And hoppin' together!)

Sleigh bells ring, are you list'nin'?
In the lane snow is glist'nin',
A beautiful sight,
We're happy tonight,
Walkin' in a winter wonderland!

Gone away is the bluebird
Here to stay is a new bird;
He sings a love song
As we go along,
Walkin' in a winter wonderland!

In the meadow we can build a snowman,
Then pretend that he is Parson Brown;
He'll say, "Are you married?"
We'll say, "No, man!
But you can do the job
While you're in town!"

Later on we'll conspire
As we dream by the fire,
To face unafraid,
The plans that we made,
Walkin' in a winter wonderland!

Sleigh bells ring, are you list'nin'?
In the lane snow is glist'nin',
A beautiful sight,
We're happy tonight,
Walkin' in a winter wonderland!

Gone away is the blue bird!
Here to stay is a new bird;
He's singing a song
As we go along,
Walkin' in a winter wonderland.

In the meadow we can build a snowman,
And pretend that he's a circus clown;
We'll have lots of fun
With Mister Snowman,
Until the other kiddies knock 'im down!

When it snows, ain't it thrillin',
Tho' your nose gets a chillin'?
We'll frolic and play
The eskimo way,
Walkin' in a winter wonderland.

Bibliography

A — Books

1   *The Alfred Burt Christmas Carols*, Alfred Burt; Hollis Music, Inc., New York, 1966

2   *Almanac of Famous People*, Vols. 1 & 2, Gale Research, Inc., Detroit, 1994

3   *ASCAP Biographical Dictionary*, Fourth Edition, Jaques Cattell Press, R.R. Bowker Co., New York, 1980

4   *Baker's Biographical Dictionary of Musicians*, Sixth Edition, Edited by Nicholas Slonimsky, Schirmer Books, New York, 1978

5   *Ballads, Carols and Tragic Legends from Southern Appalachia*, John Jacob Niles; G. Schirmer, Inc., New York, 1937

6   *Biographical Dictionary of American Music*, Charles Eugene Clagborn; Parker Publishing Co., West Nyack, New York, 1985

7   *Carols, the Joy of Christmas*, Edward Heath; Sedgwick & Jackson Ltd., London, 1977

8   *The Christmas Almanack*, Gerard and Patricia Del Re, Doubleday & Company, Inc., Garden City, New York, 1979

9   *Christmas Around the World*, New Orchard Editions Ltd., Robert Rogers House, Blanford Press Ltd., 1985 Edition

10   *Christmas Carols: A Reference Guide*, William E. Studwell; Garland Publishing, Inc., New York & London, 1985

11   *Christmas Carols and Hymns, for School and Choir*, Hollis Dann; American Book Co., New York, 1910

12   *Christmas Carols and Their Stories*, Compiled by Christopher Idle; Lion Publishing Corp., Batavia, Illinois and Sutherland, Australia, 1988

13   *Christmas Songs and Their Stories*, Herbert H. Wernecke; The Westminster Press, Philadelphia, 1957

14   *Heritage of Music: Volume 4—Music in the Twentieth Century*, Edited by Michael Raeburn and Alan Kendall, Oxford University Press, New York, 1990

15   *The International Book of Christmas Carols*, Walter Ehret and George Evans; Prentice-Hall, Inc.; Englewood Cliffs, New Jersey, 1963

16   *Irving Berlin*, Michael Freedland; Stein and Day, New York, 1974

17   *Joel Whitburn's Pop Memories 1890-1954: The History of American Popular Music*, Joel Whitburn; Record Research, Inc., Menomonee Falls, Wisconsin, 1986

18   *Joel Whitburn's Pop Singles Annual 1955-1986*, Joel Whitburn; Record Research, Inc., Menomonee Falls, Wisconsin, 1987

19 *Let's Sing Out in Ukrainian, Vol. 1*, Compiled and edited by Yurko Foty; Canuk Publications, Saskatoon, Canada, 1977

20 *New Catholic Hymnal*, Compiled and edited by Anthony Petti and Geoffrey Laycock; St. Martin's Press, New York, 1971

21 *The New Grove Dictionary of American Music, 4 Vols.*, Edited by H. Wiley Hitchcock and Stanley Sadie; MacMillan Press Limited, London, 1986

22 *The New Grove Dictionary of Music & Musicians, Vols. I-XX*, Edited by Stanley Sadie; MacMillan Publishers Limited, London, 1980

23 *The Oxford Book of Carols*, Edited by Hugh Keyte and Andrew Parrott; Oxford University Press, London and New York, 1994

24 *The Pageantry of Christmas*, Edited by Norman P. Ross; Time Inc., Book Division, 1963

25 *The Poetical Works of Henry Wadsworth Longfellow*, Household Edition, The Riverside Press, Houghton Mifflin and Company, Boston, 1885

26 *The Reader's Digest Merry Christmas Songbook*, Edited by William L. Simon; The Reader's Digest Association, Inc., Pleasantville, New York, 1981

27 *Saints for All Seasons*, Victor J. Green; Avenel Books, New York, 1982

28 *The Season for Singing: American Christmas Songs and Carols*, Compiled by John Langstaff; Doubleday & Co., Inc., Garden City, New York, 1974

29 *The Star of Bethlehem*, Frederic E. Weatherly; Hildesheimer & Faulkner, London, c.1887

30 *Ten Christmas Carols from the Southern Appalachian Mountains*, John Jacob Niles; G. Schirmer, Inc., New York, 1935. From *Schirmer's American Folk Song Series, Set 16*.

31 *Today's Missal: Advent/Ordinary Time*, Edited by Bari Colomari; Oregon Press, Portland, Oregon, 1994

32 *The Treasury of Christmas Carols*, Edited by W.L. Reed; Emerson Books, Inc., Blanford Press Ltd., England, 1961

33 *A Treasury of Christmas Songs & Carols*, Henry W. Simon; Houghton Mifflin Co., Boston, 1973

34 *Winter Wonderland, Plus 12 Golden Christmas Songs*, Edited by Bill Radics; Columbia Picture Publications, Hialeah, Florida, 1976

B — Audio Recording Jackets, Inserts, & Booklets

1 *American Colonial Christmas Music*, Berkeley Chamber Singers, Alden Gilchrist, Director & Organ, The Musical Heritage Society/MHS 1126; notes by Ida Tobias

2 *A Child Is Born*, The Kenneth Jewell Chorale, Detroit, Michigan, The Musical Heritage Society/MHS Stereo 3905, 1982; notes by Dalos Grobe

3 *Christmas in the New World*, The Western Wind Singers, The Musical Heritage Society/MHS 4077, 1979; notes by Lawrence Bennett

4 *Hallé Christmas*, Hallé Orchestra and Choir, Manchester, England, The Musical Heritage Society/MHC 6805M, 1983; notes by Philip Radcliffe

5 *Should Auld Acquaintance Be Forgot*, Kenneth Cooper and several vocalists, The Musical Heritage Society/312415A, 1989; notes by Kenneth Cooper

6 *The Unforgettable Nat King Cole*, The Reader's Digest Association, Inc./TRD147, Pleasantville, New York, 1979

C — Sheet Music Sources

1 *Carol, Brothers, Carol*, William Augustus Muhlenberg; Roy Ringwald, Arranger; Shawness Press, Inc., Delaware Water Gap, Pennsylvania, 1958

2 *Christmas Eve in My Hometown*, Don Upton and Stan Zabka; Broadcast Music, Inc., New York, Library of Congress Music Division

3 *The Christmas Waltz*, Jule Styne; Barton Music Corp., USA, 1951; Library of Congress Music Division

4 *A Cradle in Bethlehem*, Larry Stock and Alfred Bryan; Comet Music Corp., New York, 1960; Library of Congress Music Division

5 *Do You Hear What I Hear?*, N. Regney and C. Shayne; Regent Music Corp., New York, 1962; Library of Congress Music Division

6 *Mary Had a Baby*, William Dawson; Tuskegee Institute, Alabama, 1947; Library of Congress Music Division

7 *'Twas the Night Before Christmas*, Clement Clarke Moore; Ken Darby; Harry Simeone arrangement; Shawnee Press, Inc., Delaware Water Gap, Pennsylvania, 1942

D — Other Sources

1 Information provided by Michael Marks, c/o St. Nicholas Music, Inc., August 14, 1989

2 Correspondence from Wihla Hutson, August 10, 1989

3 English text provided by Mormon Tabernacle Choir, August 3, 1989

4 English text and information provided by Mary Jane Broadhurst, wife of Cecil Broadhurst, November 26, 1989

5 Newspaper article titled "Fa La La! 'Tis the Season to Be Warmed by the Undying Music of Christmas Past and Present", Connie Lauerman, *The Chicago Tribune Magazine*, December 23, 1990

6   Newspaper article titled "Show in the Skies Isn't Over Yet; Tune in As Venus Passes Jupiter", Fred Schaaf, *The Atlantic City Press,* June 16, 1991

7   Information provided by Louise Panczner from her church publication *The Weekly Bridge,* Edition of January 19, 1992

8   English text provided by the Mormon Tabernacle Choir, January 26, 1993

9   Information provided by Carl Michaelson of Carl Fischer Music Publishers, December 16, 1993

10   Correspondence from Richard and Frances Roots Hadden, February 8, 1994

11   Obituary for Jule Styne, *The Philadelphia Inquirer,* September 21, 1994

12   Newspaper article titled "A Hail to Hale for Thanksgiving", Gloria T. Delamar, *The Philadelphia Inquirer,* November 24, 1994

13   English text provided by Mormon Tabernacle Choir, July 26, 1995

14   *Arts & Entertainment* (A&E) television program titled "Santa Claus", December 25, 1995

15   CD-ROM, *Encarta Multimedia Encyclopedia,* Microsoft Corp., 1993

16   Information provided by Jaroslawa Gerulak and Lavrentia Trukewicz, and others, including librarian Natalia Palidvor-Sonevytsky, and musicologists Ihor Sonevytsky and Roman Savytsky, June 9, 2000

Song Copyright Credits

BLUE CHRISTMAS
Words & Music by Billy Hayes and Jay W. Johnson. © 1948 UNIVERSAL-POLYGRAM INTERNATIONAL PUBLISHING, INC. Copyright Renewed. All Rights Reserved.

CAROL OF THE BELLS
Words by Peter J. Wilhousky. © CARL FISCHER, INC. Copyright Renewed. International Copyright Secured. All Rights Reserved. Used by Permission.

CAROLING, CAROLING
Words by Wihla Hutson & Music by Alfred Burt. TRO © Copyright 1954 (Renewed) 1957 (Renewed) HOLLIS MUSIC, INC., New York, NY. Used by Permission.

A CHRISTMAS CAROL
By Charles Ives. © 1935 MERION MUSIC, INC. Reprinted by Permission of the Publisher.

CHRISTMAS EVE IN MY HOME TOWN
Words & Music by Stan Zabka and Don Upton. © 1951 BIG ISLAND MUSIC, INC., New York, NY. International Copyright Secured. Copyright renewed. All Rights Reserved, including public performances for profit. Used by Permission.

CHRISTMAS IN KILLARNEY
Words and Music by John Redmond, James Cavanaugh and Frank Weldon. © 1950 WARNER BROS. INC. Copyright Renewed and assigned to WARNER BROS. INC., RANGE ROAD MUSIC INC. and QUARTET MUSIC INC. All Rights Reserved. Used by Permission.

THE CHRISTMAS SONG (Chestnuts Roasting on an Open Fire)
Music and Lyric by Mel Torme and Robert Wells. © 1946 (Renewed) EDWIN H. MORRIS & COMPANY, a Division of MPL Communications, Inc. All Rights Reserved.

THE CHRISTMAS WALTZ
Words by Sammy Cahn & Music by Jule Styne. © 1954 SANDS MUSIC CORP. Copyright Renewed and Assigned to CAHN MUSIC COMPANY and JULE STYNE. All Rights on behalf of CAHN MUSIC COMPANY Administered by WB MUSIC CORP. Jule Styne's interest controlled by PRODUCERS MUSIC PUB. CO. and Administered by CHAPPELL & CO. All Rights Reserved. Used by Permission.

COWBOY CAROL
Words & Music from "The Cowboy Christmas" by Cecil Broadhurst. Copyright © THE OXFORD GROUP. Used by permission of OXFORD UNIVERSITY PRESS. All Rights Reserved.

A CRADLE IN BETHLEHEM
Words & Music by Larry Stock & Alfred Bryan. Copyright © 1952 SONY/ATV TUNES LLC. All rights administered by SONY/ATV MUSIC PUBLISHING, 8 Music Square West, Nashville, TN 37203. All Rights Reserved. Used by Permission.

DO YOU HEAR WHAT I HEAR?
Words & Music by Gloria Shayne and Noel Regney. © 1962 REGENT MUSIC CORPORATION. Copyright Renewed by JEWEL MUSIC PUBLISHING CO., INC. All Rights Reserved. Used by Permission. International Copyright Secured.

FROSTY THE SNOWMAN
Words & Music by Steve Nelson and Jack Rollins. © 1950 CHAPPELL & CO. Copyright Renewed. All Rights Reserved. Used by Permission

HAVE YOURSELF A MERRY LITTLE CHRISTMAS
Words & Music by Hugh Martin and Ralph Blane. „1943 (Renewed 1971) METRO-GOLDWYN-MAYER INC. © 1944 (Renewed 1972) EMI FEIST CATALOG INC. All Rights Controlled by EMI FEIST CATALOG INC. (Publishing) and WARNER BROS. PUBLICATIONS U.S. INC. (Print). All Rights Reserved. Used by Permission.

HERE COMES SANTA CLAUS
Words and Music by Gene Autry and Oakley Haldeman. © 1947 (Renewed 1975) WESTERN MUSIC PUBLISHING CO. All Rights Reserved. Used by Permission.

I HEARD THE BELLS ON CHRISTMAS DAY
Words by Henry Wadsworth Longfellow, adapted by Johnny Marks & Music by Johnny Marks. Copyright © 1956 (Renewed 1984) ST. NICHOLAS MUSIC, INC., New York, NY. All Rights Reserved. Used by Permission.

I WONDER AS I WANDER
Words & Music by John Jacob Niles. © 1934 (Renewed) by G. SCHIRMER, INC. (ASCAP) International Copyright Secured. All Rights Reserved. Reprinted by Permission.

I'LL BE HOME FOR CHRISTMAS
Words & Music by Kim Gannon and Walter Kent. © 1943 (Renewed) by GANNON & KENT MUSIC CO., INC., Beverly Hills, CA. Copyright Renewed. International Copyright Secured. All Rights Reserved.

Notes

To understand Keys to Notes, please refer to the Bibliography, pages 133-136.

A numbers refer to **Books**

B numbers refer to **Audio Recording Jackets, Inserts, and Booklets**

C numbers refer to **Sheet Music**

D numbers refer to **Other Sources**

The Historical Perspective

A27
D15

Carols

1	Away in a Manger	A10,13,14,21,23,31
2	The Birthday of a King	A10,11,33
3	Blue Christmas	A2,3,6,21,26
4	Carol, Brothers, Carol	A2,21,22 C1 D12
5	Carol of the Bells	A10,19,21,24 D9,16
6	Caroling, Caroling	A1 B2 D2
7	A Christmas Carol	A10,13 B3
8	Christmas Eve in My Home Town	A3 C2
9	Christmas in Killarney	A2,3,10,14
10	The Christmas Song	A3,26 B6
11	The Christmas Waltz	A3,10 C3
12	Cowboy Carol	A3,10,32 B4 D4,10
13	A Cradle in Bethlehem	A3 C4
14	Do You Hear What I Hear?	A2,3 C5
15	Frosty the Snow Man	A3,8,17,21,26
16	Go Tell It on the Mountain	A2,12,13,26,31
17	Have Yourself a Merry Little Christmas	A3,26
18	Here Comes Santa Claus	A3,17,21,26
19	I Heard the Bells on Christmas Day	A3,15,25 D1
20	I Wonder As I Wander	A5,10,21,23,30
21	I'll Be Home for Christmas	A3,17,21,26 D5
22	It Came Upon the Midnight Clear	A8,10,12,15 D5
23	It's Beginning to Look Like Christmas	A2,3,4,10,26
24	Jesus, Jesus, Rest Your Head	A5,7,10,28,30 D13
25	Jingle-Bell Rock	A3,8,21 D1
26	Jingle Bells	A17,21,26 B5
27	Let It Snow! Let It Snow! Let It Snow!	A3,6,10,17,26 D11
28	The Little Drummer Boy	A3,10,21
29	Mary Had a Baby	A10,12,22 B2 C6
30	O Little Town of Bethlehem	A8,10,15
31	Rockin' Around the Christmas Tree	A3,18,21 D1
32	Rudolph the Red-Nosed Reindeer	A3,6,17,18,21 D1,5
33	Santa Claus Is Comin' to Town	A3,8,10,17,21,26
34	The Shepherd's Carol	A10,14,22 B1
35	The Shepherd's Story	A22 D3
36	Silver Bells	A3,22

Translator

A Winter Sleigh Ride
c.1840, oil on canvas
Thomas Birch (1779-1851)
Brandywine River Museum

Title Index

Audio Index

	Title	Performed By
CD 1	The Shepherd's Carol	Catherdral Choir of St. John the Divine
	Star in the East	The Western Wind Singers
	Mary Had a Baby	The Riverside Choir; Timothy Smith, Director of Music & Organist; Helen Cha-Pyo, Associate Director & Conductor.
	It Came Upon a Midnight Clear	Mormon Tabernacle Choir; Richard P. Condie, director
	We Three Kings of Orient Are	Robert Shaw Chamber Singers/Ronald Burrichter, tenor; Victor Ledbetter, baritone; Wayne Baughman, bass
	Go Tell It on the Mountain	The Westminster Choir College; Joseph Flummerfelt, conductor; Daniel Beckwith, organist; Nancy Tenore, soprano; Jeffrey Martin, tenor
	I Heard the Bells on Christmas Day	Kate Smith; Arranged & conducted by Peter Matz
	O Little Town of Bethlehem	Ray Price
	Away in a Manger	Tanya Tucker
	The Birthday of a King	James McCracken
	A Christmas Carol	The Western Wind Singers
	The Shepherd's Story	Mormon Tabernacle Choir/Alexander Schreiner & Frank Asper, organ
	Caroling, Caroling	Fred Waring & The Pennsylvanians
	Carol, Brothers, Carol	Fred Waring & The Pennsylvanians
CD 2	Carol of the Bells	Mormon Tabernacle Choir/The Columbia Symphony Orchestra; Jerold Ottley, director
	Jesus, Jesus, Rest Your Head	The Mariners
	I Wonder As I Wander	Mahlia Jackson; Orchestra under the direction of Sid Bass
	The Little Drummer Boy	The Harry Simeone Chorale
	Cowboy Carol	Hallé Orchestra & Chorus
	The Star Carol	"Tennessee" Ernie Ford
	Some Children See Him	Andy Williams; Arranged & conducted by Robert Mersey
	A Cradle in Bethlehem	Nat "King" Cole
	Do You Hear What I Hear?	Andy Williams; Arranged & conducted by Robert Mersey

'Twas the Night Before Christmas	Fred Waring & The Pennsylvanians
Jingle Bells	Burl Ives
Toyland	Perry Como with the Ray Charles Singers; Arranged & conducted by Nick Perito
Santa Claus Is Comin' to Town	Willie Nelson
Winter Wonderland	Johnny Mathis with Percy Faith & his Orchestra
White Christmas	Bing Crosby
I'll Be Home for Christmas	Chet Akins
Have Yourself a Merry Little Christmas	Andy Williams; Arranged & conducted by Robert Mersey

CD 3

Let It Snow! Let It Snow! Let It Snow!	Woody Herman & his Orchestra
The Christmas Song	Nat "King" Cole
Here Comes Santa Claus	Gene Autry with vocal group
Blue Christmas	Tammy Wynette
Sleigh Ride (Parish-Anderson)	Mormon Tabernacle Choir/The Columbia Symphony Orchestra; Jerold Ottley, director
Rudolph the Red-Nosed Reindeer	Gene Autry and The Pinafores with orchestral accompaniment
Christmas in Killarney	Bing Crosby
Frosty the Snow Man	Gene Autry with The Cass County Boys; Orchestra conducted by Carl Cotner
It's Beginning to Look Like Christmas	Kate Smith; Arranged & conducted by Peter Matz
There Is No Christmas Like a Home Christmas	Perry Como with the Ray Charles Singers; Arranged & conducted by Nick Perito
Christmas Eve in My Home Town	Kate Smith; Arranged & conducted by Peter Matz
Silver Bells	Mormon Tabernacle Choir/The Columbia Symphony Orchestra; Jerold Ottley, director
The Christmas Waltz	Robert Goulet
Jingle-Bell Rock	Bobby Helms
Rockin' Around the Christmas Tree	Brenda Lee
What Are You Doing New Year's Eve?	Johnny Mathis; Arranged & conducted by Ernie Freeman